KRISHNANANDA TROBE, M.D,
WITH AMANA TROBE

Stepping *Out of* Fear

BREAKING FREE
OF OUR PAIN
AND SUFFERING

Copyright © 2013 by Krishnananda Trobe and Amana Trobe
All rights reserved.

ISBN-10: 1481009923
ISBN-13: 9781481009928

DEDICATION:

We would like to dedicate this book to everyone who takes the rewarding and sometimes arduous journey of self-discovery and stepping out of fear.

TABLE OF CONTENTS

INTRODUCTION: 1

PART 1 – THE OVERVIEW

Chapter 1: THE EMOTIONAL CHILD STATE OF MIND   11

Chapter 2: THE BUBBLE   21

Chapter 3: THE MIRROR   33

PART 2 – THE EMOTIONAL CHILD IN ACTION

Chapter 4: REACTIONS AND CONTROL   43

Chapter 5: EXPECTATIONS AND ENTITLEMENT   53

Chapter 6: COMPROMISE   65

Chapter 7: ADDICTIVENESS   75

Chapter 8: MAGICAL THINKING   85

PART 3 – THE INNER EXPERIENCE OF THE EMOTIONAL CHILD

Chapter 9: EMPTINESS AND NEEDINESS   93

Chapter 10: FEAR   103

Chapter 11: THE INFECTIONS   113

Chapter 12: SHAME AND GUILT   121

Chapter 13: THE PUSHER-JUDGE 135

Chapter 14: SHOCK 145

Chapter 15: ABANDONMENT, DEPRIVATION, AND NEGLECT 153

Chapter 16: ENGULFMENT 169

Chapter 17: MISTRUST AND ANGER 181

PART 4 – BREAKING FREE

Chapter 18: BREAKING FREE OF OLD PATTERNS 191

Chapter 19: DEALING WITH PAINFUL EMOTIONS 203

Chapter 20: STANDING UP FOR OURSELVES 209

Chapter 21: REPRESSION, EXPRESSION AND CONTAINMENT 221

Chapter 22: SEX AND THE EMOTIONAL CHILD 235

Chapter 23: BREAKING OUT OF THE PRISON OF ROLES 245

Chapter 24: RELATING AND THE EMOTIONAL CHILD 257

Chapter 25: LIVING IN BALANCE 271

CONCLUSION 279

Selected References 285

Introduction:

(This is the second edition of this book. I (Krish) wrote the first edition alone, but since then, Amana and I have been working together leading seminars around the world. We have created *The Learning Love Institute*, have developed and refined *The Learning Love Work*, and we are now training teachers in many countries to lead our seminars and give sessions based on this work. In this edition, which we rewrote together, although the personal experiences are still from my life, the material reflects what we teach in our seminars, and individual and couples work.)

It strikes us that one of the deepest questions we face is how to break the old patterns that keep us from experiencing aliveness, love, and joy. This is particularly true in our relating, but it also affects our creativity, our sexuality and other aspects of our life. This is the question that we address in this book.

Much of the problem lies with how we see ourselves. When I (Krish) was a child, one of my favorite movies was *"Hans Christian Anderson"* with Danny Kaye. My parents bought us a recording of the songs and we sang them all the time. One was the song, "There Once Was An Ugly Duckling," a story of a very ugly little duck "with feathers all ruffled and brown" that was ostracized from his world of ducks because he didn't fit in. He was forced to wander until one day, he found himself with some swans and discovered that he was really a very beautiful swan who just happened to be born among ducks.

In a sense, we are on a journey to rediscover our "swanness"- our real selves. We have deluded ourselves into believing that we are "ducks". "Ducks" basically feel and see themselves as frightened, ugly, unloved, and unlovable creatures living in a strange and unfriendly world where no one really appreciates and sees them. And, they cover up their fears and insecurities with all manner of compensations. Stressed out, driven, competitive little "ducks", covered up with false masks. "Swans "feel and see themselves as lively, capable, gifted beings, flowing naturally with their life energy and contributing their love and unique creativity.

In our first book, *Face To Face With Fear*, I (Krish) shared my experiences of working with my own fears as a road to deeper vulnerability and self-acceptance. I have felt that penetrating deeply into the wounds of the inner child was a road to creating love in our life - love for ourselves and love with others. I spent years exploring this inner woundedness, a space that I previously had ignored and pushed down. I came to see that when these wounds are not conscious, they sabotage our life and our love in all manner of ways. Exploring our wound in depth, being aware of them, and feeling them as body experiences is still one of the cornerstones of our work. But this kind of exploration is only the first step on the journey. Without the second step, it is possible to get lost in these wounds because what stands between us and love and joy is not just that we have unhealed wounds but that *we are identified with them.*

> *We repeat our old patterns because we carry a wounded self–image and we believe that this is who we are. We are identified with a wounded "emotional child" inside.*

We refer to this space as "an emotional child" because it is driven by powerful emotions that are beyond our control or often beyond our consciousness. As long as we are caught in this identification, we are out of control and driven by fear. We are like a car being driven by a young, impetuous, uncentered child or by a way of living that covers up our insecurities and fears. We have no choice but to keep repeating old patterns and attract people and situations that support the ways we see ourselves.

The second step in my own journey has been realizing that this emotional child is not who I am. I have been strongly identified with a self-image and inner feeling of being a younger brother who could never match up to an older brother whom I perceived as more intelligent, charismatic, self-confident and even more sensitive and considerate than I was. I also perceived that he was always getting the attention and the respect that I craved and that everyone, including my parents, deferred to him. I have explored every conceivable aspect of this wound. Yet the shame, fears and insecurities remained. In certain situations, I would be totally overtaken by this experience and be helpless to do anything about it except to watch it. All efforts to change it or get rid of it have never worked. Countless times, I would even sabotage my performance in situations where I felt under stress.

For a long time, I had no sense that I would or could be anything other than this role. It felt like this was basically who I was and all efforts to escape it were simply covers. I remember one poignant moment in my life that brought this home to me very strongly. My brother was a junior at Harvard University. I was applying for acceptance. One day, the letter arrived from the Dean of Admissions and when I opened it, I was stunned to see that I had been accepted. My reaction was that there had to have been some mistake. Later, I learned that the Dean has told my brother who by then was one of the editors of the Harvard Crimson, that "if your brother is half as good as you are, we will take him."

The self-image of a younger brother who basically was only half as good had haunted me all my life. Yet there came a time in my inner exploration that I began to realize that this is not who I am. I gradually began to recognize that this self-image came as a result of a very powerful conditioning. By moving out of the family net, finding a very different life and world for myself and developing my own gifts and meditation, I came to see that this self-concept was just a product of the past.

Strangely enough, I was so blinded by this perception of myself that I could not even see my unique gifts. As my sense of myself shifted, so did my life. Many of the old behaviors that so powerfully affected my relating, my creativity, and my joy in the past became less and less significant. Now, there are still some moments when the old sense of myself takes over my consciousness. But the difference is that I am aware of it, I can watch it from a distance, and it passes.

It is not easy to recognize our "swanness" because our identification with our "duckness" is very deep. It began at a time when we were just beginning to from a self-concept.

> *We base our sense of self on the values of those who cared for us and the society and culture we were raised in. We learn to cut off from ourselves. This is the basis of what we call the "emotional child" or "the wounded child"- an inner experience of self that is full of fear, shame and mistrust and covered with compulsive and unconscious behaviors.*

When our emotional child drives our life, it can show itself in many ways:

- One way is that we find ourselves *repeating the same painful patterns* in our relationships again and again without understanding why.
- Another is that we project out and attempt to *live up to a false "elevated" image of ourselves.*
- Another is that we may become *lost in addictive behavior* of one kind or other.
- Another is that we may have repetitive *accidents or illnesses* or sabotage out life repeatedly.
- Still another is that we easily feel *resigned, discouraged, hopeless and depressed.*
- And finally, we habitually get *angry, pull away, please, or rescue* when we are disturbed.

It has been extremely helpful for me to explore, feel and understand the wounds that I carried inside. But at a certain point, I realized that my focus was naturally shifting toward watching the moments when I am being taken over by my emotional child. I have become much less concerned with what happened in the past and more focused on watching how this emotional child affects my day-to-day life now. We also notice this as a natural shift in the people that we work with in our trainings. Once they have become intimately connected with the wounds inside, (by that we mean not just an intellectual connection but a visceral one), the focus moves toward the present.

And, focusing on the present means seeing how and when we become identified with their emotional child and how that affects our life. It means noticing how we can be overcome with shame, fear or mistrust at any moment and behave as a child behaves - reactive, complaining, compromising, compensating, or losing ourselves in some kind of addiction.

About twenty-five years ago, after spending many years pursuing different spiritual paths, I went to India and became the disciple of an enlightened spiritual Master. Amana came some years later and that is where we got together. We have followed his unique path of self-discovery quite intensively and passionately during the years. This path has essentially involved learning to bring awareness to our lives and learning to be present to the moment in an atmosphere of playfulness and celebration.

When I went to India, even though I was in relationship, I had little idea of what love meant or what it meant to be close to someone. I was much too busy with myself, with my work and with making sure that I "did my own thing". But over these years, I have learned a bit more about how to love.

The approach that we present here is a very specific method for watching and understanding how the emotional child operates in our life. This can be challenging because it has such a powerful hold on our feelings and behavior. When this part of us grips us, there is often little space to observe. We move from trigger to reaction in record time. In this method, there is no goal to change or fix anything but simply to watch and allow what is there. This process slowly releases us from the control and the fear of this inner part of us. As we come to understand how it runs our life, we transcend its influence and we begin to have choices. We are no longer out of control or driven by fear.

Our approach is based on some simple truths:
1. *We are in pain and suffering because our life, thinking and body experience is being run by a deeply wounded, insecure, mistrustful and frightened part of us, a part we call, "the emotional child".*
2. *We are identified with this part of us – we believe that it is who we are.*
3. *To dis-identify from this emotional child and take back our life, we need to get to know this part of us, feel the pain and fear it carries and finally begin to take risks that help us to break out of old habits and ways of living.*

Each chapter covers an area that I have explored in my own inner search and we offer many examples from my own life. We cite examples from friends and participants in our work but of course, have changed the names and some of the circumstances to protect confidentiality. We have made the chapters as concise and simple as possible and followed each with specific exercises to facilitate everyone's own exploration.

We are painting with broad strokes. Each chapter is not meant to be a definitive discussion of the topic. We provide references of great books that have helped us if you wish to go deeper with each topic. Our intention is to give an overview of both the behavior and the inner experience of the emotional child so that you have the tools to be present when it arises and at the same time, recognize that it is not who you are. Our suggestion as you read the book is to take your time. It is written a bit like a workbook and each chapter deals with a different aspect of your life. It can take time to digest each section.

> " The real juice of life is within you.
> This very moment you can turn within yourself,
> Look into yourself.
> No worship is needed; it is a silent journey to your own being.
> And the moment you find your own center,
> You have found the center of the whole existence."
> Osho

Part 1:
WHAT IS TRUST?

Chapter 1:

THE EMOTIONAL CHILD STATE OF MIND

Let's look more precisely at this "emotional child". Imagine that a little boy walks into your room right now and asks you if you could go out and play with him. You have some important work to do and you just can't spend the time this moment to play with him. He begins to make a fuss. You would like him to understand that you can play with him tomorrow but today, you just can't. Tomorrow means nothing to him and he stamps his feet and says, "NO! NOW!" Then he begins to cry and throw a tantrum.

We have a part of us inside that is just like this little boy - a space which has no concept of tomorrow that does not like to wait and does not like to be disappointed. It cannot defer gratification of pleasure until another time because it does not believe that there is another time. And, it has no space inside to deal with pain or discomfort. For each of us, our behavior may be a bit different, but the deeper experience of this lack of inner space is much the same for all of us. This is what we could call "a wounded child state of mind" or "an emotional child" space inside. In this state of consciousness, we have no ability whatsoever to be with what is, to stay present and contain experience. When we are in this frame of mind, we are basically frightened, mistrustful and full of insecurity. These fears make us impulsive, reactive, perpetually restless, or profoundly shocked and frozen.

Normally, when we are in this frame of mind, we are not aware that there is anything else about us except this space. We become totally identified with this emotional child and we don't have a clue that it is not who we are. Because of deep unhealed childhood wounds, most of us have always been full of fear, shame, and mistrust. We have created a self-identity based on this emotional child. But these qualities are not part of our true nature; they have been instilled as a result of our conditioning and as a result of experiences over which we had no control.

We sometimes show a movie in our seminars by Roman Polanski called *"Bitter Moon"*. It depicts what happens when two people enter into a relationship and both are living in the child state of mind without awareness. The film is a story of a love affair gone bad. The first part shows the unconsciousness of two people falling in love both convinced that they have finally found the love that they are seeking. For a while, they enjoy a honeymoon of intense passion and loving feelings for each other. But as their relating deepens, each one compromises more and more and becomes resentful of the other. At first, one tyrannizes the other and then they change roles. The ending is a bit over-dramatic but it shows that love without awareness only leads to pain.

Two Aspects of the Emotional Child
In our own explorations, we have discovered when we penetrated deeply into this emotional child state, that there are two aspects to it. The first, which is in front, are *the acting out behaviors* that run our life when we are in the grips of our emotional child. These are:

1. Reaction and Control
2. Expectation and Entitlement
3. Compromise
4. Addictiveness
5. Magical Thinking

These are five faces that another meets when he or she encounters and gets to know us. Behind these behaviors is another, deeper, part that is *the feelings* of this wounded child state of mind. They are:

1. Fear and Shock
2. Shame, Guilt, and Insecurity
3. Neediness and Emptiness
4. Sadness and Grief
5. Mistrust and Anger

THE EMOTIONAL CHILD STATE OF MIND

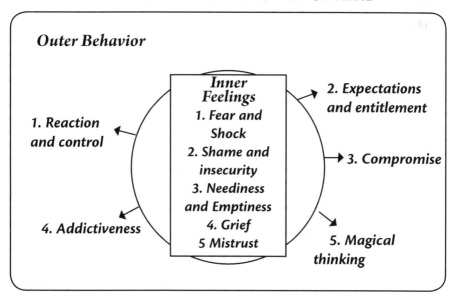

Five Behaviors of the Emotional Child
We will mention a bit about each of the five behaviors and feelings now but will go into much more detail in subsequent chapters. In the child state of mind, we *react* quiet automatically to the events of our life.

> *Our reactions are driven by the fears that unless we react, something bad will happen or we will never get what we need. We move automatically from trigger to reaction without any awareness of what is happening or why. And the space between the trigger and the reaction is infinitesimal.*

We react so quickly and so automatically because we feel that it is a matter or life and death. Every time. We react whenever we feel threatened. We react to get our needs met. We react on the other person whenever we don't feel safe, loved and appreciated. When two people approach each other in the child state of mind, they each see in the other person either someone who must meet his or her unfulfilled needs or someone who could hurt him or her in some way. As a result, they both compulsively attempt to control the other in all manner of ways. What follows is conflict, unfulfilled expectations, miscommunication, power games, and pain.

The child inside of us also *expects* - from others and from life. He or she expects that his needs will be met and that his discomfort and fears will be taken away. It is natural that a child would feel this way because in his or her helplessness and insecurity, how else can he or she hope to feel safe?

Sometimes we have experienced so many disappointments that our expectations become buried in resignation. But they are still there, lurking in the longings of our emotional child.

For some of us, this expecting aspect of our child state of mind can be right out front. We feel entitled. People owe us! We demand, blame, or feel righteously hurt when things don't go our way or when we feel deprived of attention. For others of us, our expectations are more covert, covered with denial and pretense. But dig a little, and out they come. And nothing brings them out so well as coming closer to someone.

It is also natural that when we are in fear and shame – based in our child state of mind, we live a life of *compromise*. Shame and fear leads to compromise because we are terrified of what others will think and we have lost touch with our own strength and self-confidence. Furthermore, we don't trust our own thoughts, feelings and institution. In short, we live not for ourselves but for others.

When we are in the grip of our child state of mind, we are also highly prone to *addiction*. We want instant relief and instant gratification as does any child. If we don't have much ability to watch and get space from our feelings and fears, we easily run to all kinds of addictive behavior. When the anxiety or fear arises, we unconsciously reach for something to soothe us. Often these addictions are chronic and we are not even aware that they are there or what drives them. But if we could have some comprehension for how terrified our emotional child is inside, we would probably have much more compassion for our addictiveness.

Finally, when we are in this child state of mind, we *magically hope* that the right person will come along who will take away all our fear and pain. We hope to be relieved of our loneliness, fears and pain. With friends and lovers, we try to change them to make them as we want to them to be or we go to another person with the hope that this one will finally live up to our expectations. Either way, we don't have to feel the pain of aloneness when they disappoint us. Our emotional child cannot see things as they are because he or she idealizes. He or she needs to feel that people and life operate in a certain way to feel safe and to make order in his inner world. So, he simply imagines that things are as he wants them to be. He sets people up on pedestals and lives in hopes and illusions.

Five Wounds of the Emotional Child
It is easier to recognize the behaviors of our emotional child. To uncover the feelings that lie behind these behaviors, we have to take a step deeper. The *fears* are deeply rooted in our minds and are based on earlier experiences, many of which we may no longer remember. Furthermore, because the child state is wounded, when we are in this state, we don't feel free or spontaneous, we experience ourselves as full of *shame, unworthiness and inferiority* and full of *sadness, anger and mistrust*. We don't feel self-sufficient; on the contrary, we feel *empty* and desperately *long* for someone to fill us up. We compulsively look to the outside for inner well-being.

Normally, we are highly identified with this child state of mind. When it grips our consciousness, which can happen anytime we feel the slightest frustration, deprivation, or disturbance, it feels that this is totally who we are. It is hard to imagine when we are lost in our reactions, buried in expectations, or overwhelmed with insecurity and fear, that it is only an emotional child inside of us that has taken over.

CHAPTER 1: THE EMOTIONAL CHILD STATE OF MIND

The most significant message of our spiritual teacher, whose work has been such a powerful inspiration to us, has always been to learn to watch. Meditation, he said, is the one and only medicine that he had for us. It is the treatment for everything that ails us. This watching applies to every aspect of our life.

For understanding our difficulties in relating, our damaged self-esteem and much of our behavior patterns, it also means learning to watch our emotional child in all his or her forms. We each have inside of us this ability to watch, contain, and understand but it takes practice to develop this skill. At first, we live mostly in our child state of mind and there is little or no observing happening. We move from trigger to reaction as a robot without understanding why we behave and feel as we do. It is automatic, unconscious, and habitual. But when we begin to watch and understand more about our emotional child space inside, this witnessing ability deepens. And as it deepens, our consciousness matures.

How do we get to know and embrace this child state? No differently from how we might deal with the little boy or girl who came in our room and demanded our attention. We don't repress him or her or tell him or her to go away. That only creates trouble because he will just go somewhere else and act out. Or she may fold into herself and hide all her enthusiasm and gifts, which is what many of us did.

Instead, we try to understand about this behavior and what lies behind it. We give this emotional child our love and attention. We watch him or her without judgment. This does not make it go away. But it no longer exerts such a powerful hidden force in our life that directs our feelings, thoughts, and behaviors without our awareness. There will perhaps always be a part of us inside that will remain fearful and reactive, mistrustful and insecure *but it does not have to run our lives.*

But as our watcher gets stronger and our maturity grows, we get space from it. When it takes over our consciousness, we can recognize that a visitor has come to stay into our house. We can watch and, taking a deep breath, let it be. These behaviors – reaction, expectations, addiction, and compensations – are symptoms of deeper feelings underneath. By gently practicing to be with them rather than judge them, we can also recognize and "be with "the feelings of mistrust, fear, emptiness and insecurity that are behind the behaviors.

Understanding about the emotional child state of mind explains a great deal about our life. We come to understand how and why we react, why we have so much fear inside, why we are so hungry for love and attention or why it is so hard to allow someone to come close. We also come to understand why we are so full of shame and mistrust, why we are so restless, why we have problems in expressing ourselves in our sexuality, in our creativity, or in our ability to express and assert ourselves. In short, it gives us insights into much of our daily life.

Everybody wants to be loved.
That is a wrong beginning.
And it starts because the child, the small child,
Cannot love, cannot say anything, cannot do
Anything, cannot give anything - he can only get.
A small child's experience of love is of getting.
But the trouble arises because
Everybody has been a child, and
Everybody has the same urge to get love;
And nobody is born in any other way.
So all are asking, "Give us love,"
And there is nobody to give

> *Because the other person is also*
> *Brought up in the same way."*
> Osho

Exercise:
1. Exploring the Emotional Child.

Three chief qualities of this state of mind are fear, shame, and reactivity. Reactions are the behaviors in front; shame and fear is the experience behind.

1. Begin to notice your reactivity. Notice when it arises, how it feels and what you do from this reactive state.
2. In those moments when you see and feel yourself reacting, ask yourself, "What am I afraid of or insecure about right now?"

2. Watching the Judgments of Your Child State of Mind.

1. Notice when you judge yourself for being reactive, fearful, mistrustful or full of shame.
2. How does it feel when you judge?
3. Try simply saying to yourself, "Ah, judgment is happening."

Chapter 2:

THE BUBBLE

When we are in the child state of mind, and when we are in the grips of our emotional child, it is as though we are living in a bubble. The wounded child is inside of this bubble trapped in all his or her beliefs and expectations. In this bubble, we cannot see the world outside as it is; we only see it through the filter of our beliefs and expectations.

For instance, one client was having a painful ongoing conflict with a colleague at work. She is the boss but she feels that no one listens to her. When we explored more deeply, we discovered that she had been in similar situations in her life where she has felt helpless and not respected. She has a long history of minimizing her needs and allowing people to overrun her boundaries. Inside of her bubble, she feels no strength and no right to assert her needs or limits. What she sees outside of the bubble is world of people who are stronger, clearer and more important that she is. The automatic and habitual behavior that she moves into from this space is to hold back her energy and feel horribly guilty whenever she asserts herself in any way. The reaction she gets back from others also reflects the condition of being in her bubble. They don't respect or even listen to what she has to say.

We each have our own kind of bubble with our own unique set of beliefs, negative expectations, and reactions that reflect the particular state of our woundedness. It may be immense shame and insecurity, deep shock and fear, or mistrust and loneliness. Or all of these. This gestalt can be provoked at any time. We react from our bubble state in our own unique way.

To cite another example, we had a man in a group who gets very disturbed, mistrustful, and agitated when he feels that his surroundings are not supportive and loving. Then he moves into an aggressive mode and becomes belligerent. Inside his bubble, he feels in constant threat. He looks out from this space; sees a world that is aggressive, and he has to be continually on guard and ready to defend himself at anytime. In his relationships with people, particularly his partner, the slightest hint of invasion or demand provokes this space for him. Immediately, he is inside the bubble. Naturally, people also respond to him with aggression, defense, and fear.

In the Bubble, We Are Identified with the Wound
When we are in our bubble, whatever it is, we are deeply identified with the child inside the bubble. For instance, if we are in a *shame bubble* — in other words, if we believe that we are wrong, unlovable, a failure and sinful, then that's who we think we are. *We are shame.* That is all we would see if someone were to hold a mirror in front of us. Certain situations bring up this "shame bubbleness" very strongly — for example rejection or criticism can trigger us to enter into a shame bubble.

Many of us are in a bubble all the time.

There are different bubbles, varieties of our identification with some aspect of our woundedness - mistrust, shame, abandonment, engulfment, or shock. Rarely the bubble pops and we experience ourselves out of it and then another trigger comes and we are back in it.

We pick the metaphor of a bubble for several reasons:

One reason is that it is like a prison without any doors or windows. What we believe, feel, hear, and see from our viewpoint inside the bubble seems totally true. We cannot see or hear anything else. Even if there were someone outside showering us with love, telling us that what we are believing and seeing is false, assuring us that we are loved, that the world is a safe and loving place, and we are a wonderful, creative, and precious person, we cannot hear it or take it in. We are insulated inside of our bubble. Anything from the outside can feel like an invasion.

Another reason that we pick this metaphor is that the bubble can pop at any moment. It does not take a sledgehammer or a ton of dynamite to break it down. It just takes awareness and risk. When the bubble does pop, we find ourselves outside and it is hard to believe that we were ever in it and believed, felt, or behaved in the way we did when we were taken over by this consciousness. Until we are back inside once again. Then we may have a vague memory of what it was like to be outside.

> *The understanding of this bubble phenomenon can help us to see that it is not who we are. We can begin to see that it is a state of mind that grabs us but there are moments when we are free of it. And if there are moments when we are free of this identity of shame, mistrust, and so on, then it must mean it is not who we are.*

Finally, there is another reason that we describe this phenomenon as a bubble. If we imagined that our consciousness were a circle, we could say that when we begin this process, when we go into our bubble because when something triggers it - at that moment, it fills up much of the circle. Our experience is all "bubbleness". Our shame or our mistrust, for instance, takes us over. We are so identified with the wounded child inside the bubble that we are unable to recognize that we are not this wounded child. But as our awareness deepens, as we gain more compassion and understanding for our woundedness, and as our ability to watch improves, the bubble starts to shrink. There is more and more space around the bubble, more consciousness, more ability to see and watch it, and to recognize that it is not who we really are.

Bubble Consciousness is a Hypnosis

The bubble phenomenon is a trance state, a hypnosis. Steven Wolinsky has discussed these trance phenomena in his book, <u>Trances People Live.</u> As he points out, the characteristics of this trance state are that it is not connected to reality. When we are in this trance, we do not see, hear or feel what is happening in the moment because our impressions are influenced by memories imprinted in our nervous system from an earlier time. It is as though a part of us is frozen at a time when we were traumatized and deprived of essential needs such as love, support and security. The perceptions of this wounded child inside the bubble are those of a frightened, mistrusting, shamed and needy child. When we are caught in our bubble, we believe *this is really the truth.*

Different Kinds of Bubbles
Wolinsky has a different way of describing trances than we do. We focus on how our past traumas create different kinds of bubbles. For instance, Susan, in the example mentioned above, is in what we call a *"shame bubble"*. In a *"shame bubble"*, we feel unlovable, a failure and useless. We may doubt that we have anything to share, feel that everyone else does it better, and even that we were stupid to risk putting ourselves out.

Another kind of bubble is an *"abandonment/deprivation bubble"*. Here we feel unloved and enter into a familiar dark space of feeling deprived and desperately lonely where we may even be flooded with earlier memories of being rejected and lonely. It can be provoked by a lover or friend no longer wanting to be with us or pulling away and withholding his or her love. Of course shame and abandonment go together so often it is hard to separate one from the other. But when we discuss each in greater detail later, the differences in approaching these two wounds will become clearer.

In a recent workshop in Switzerland, a woman got into an argument with one of the men who was also participating. It was a long group and all of the members had become very close and loving with each other. But at this time, she felt that he was being insensitive and aggressive. When they brought it up in the group, it came out that she had a way of being bossy that reminded him of his older sister who had tyrannized him. He, in turn, had a way of provoking women that reminded her of her angry and abusive father. This was a case of bubble meets bubble. Both had been taken over by their child state of consciousness and had entered into their respective bubbles. This actually accounts for much of the conflicts and misunderstanding that we have with others. People in relationship often relate from one wound to another.

> *Our trances or bubbles come from our woundedness. Although in a sense, we have only one wound, we will be looking at this wound from five different perspectives, mistrust, abandonment, shame, fear and engulfment, because it helps us to understand and work with them more deeply. When we enter into a bubble, it is some manifestation of these five.*

Different situations trigger different kinds of bubbles. Each bubble has characteristic feelings, beliefs and behavior, and each has a characteristic way that we see ourselves. Each has characteristic ways that it gets provoked and how life and people respond to us when we are in it. Once we know about these wounds, we can recognize when we are in a bubble by these characteristics:

- *How it feels*
- *How we behave when we are in it*
- *What triggers it*
- *The thought forms and self-identity that it provokes*

For instance, a man from one of our workshops shared that he felt he could never get enough attention or time together with his girlfriend. This made him angry and demanding. Her reaction was to become angry and pull away. When he feels deprived of her love, he enters into his deprivation/abandonment bubble. From this space, he reacts automatically and unconsciously with anger, begging, and demanding. The response he gets when he is in this bubble is the same - rejection. When we asked him how he sees and feels himself when he is in this bubble, he said that he sees someone who is helpless, alone, and desperate for love and feels that if he does not react, he will never get what he needs.

Breaking the Identification – Coming Out of the Bubble
We highlight four main ways that we come out of bubbles and begin to break our identification with our wounded child:

- *The first is having more understanding and compassion for that child in the bubble.*
- *The second is getting support from someone we can trust who helps us to see ourselves, others, and the situation objectively.*
- *The third is being willing to feel what it feels like when we are in the bubble rather running away into denial, distraction, reaction, or compensation.*
- *The fourth is by taking risks that challenge the truth of what we believe about ourselves when we are in the bubble.*

> **As the self-image that we have of ourselves when we are in this bubble starts to fade, transformation happens. We gradually stop being so easily triggered. We no longer react so compulsively and so strongly from our bubble identity and we no longer get the same responses from other people and from life.**

For instance, Susan, a person we have worked with, has believed that she is a useless, uncreative person. The slightest criticism would easily trigger her and her reaction would be to be defensive and self-sabotaging. Life and people responded to her with constant rejections that only re-enforced her negative beliefs. It was a painfully vicious spiral. By learning more about her shame (in the ways that we will discuss later), she developed more understanding and compassion for how and why she felt and believed what she did and why she would go into her bubble so easily. She was also willing to feel the shame when it came up instead of running away from it. By taking small risks to explore and express her creative gifts, she gradually began to see that she is not so powerless, useless and uncreative as she always thought. Slowly her bubble identify is fading. In this way, lifelong patterns stop repeating themselves.

When we start bringing awareness to how we live in bubbles, it also helps to get a *reality check*. In our work, we call this "coming up for air". If something has landed us into a deep shame or mistrust bubble, often checking in with a trusted friend can be enough to help us to see that what we see, feel and think is not true but tinted by our past experiences. Of course, sometimes we are so deeply in our bubble that we are not able to take anything. Then there is nothing to do but give it time. Lovers may not be the best people to go to for reality checks especially if they are the trigger of the bubble. But if there is enough trust, it is a wonderful way of deepening the love and the connection between two people.

There is simply no alternative to *feeling the fears and insecurities* that we harbor inside. We may try all kinds of ways to run away from our fears and insecurities, but they never go away until we take the decision to go in a feel them. And this step is truly transformative.

From my experience, it was not as frightening to connect with the depth of my fears and insecurity as I suspected. I was afraid that if I admitted to myself (and eventually to others) how frightened and insecure I really was inside, it would only make it worse. Actually, the opposite was true. It made me feel better to admit and to feel it. And it also made me see that I really wasn't quite as frightened and insecure as I thought. Sure, fear and insecurity was there but I also realized that I have a lot of courage and gifts. I wasn't all fear and insecurity covered with compensations.

Finally, there is the quality of risk. When we do something out of our familiar comfort zone, we challenge our old ways of being and seeing ourselves. It is a big jump to let go of our old ways of being and embrace the new, unknown and unfamiliar. Our wounded self has always been in bubbles and may never let go of all of its induced thought forms and behaviors. It is easier to believe and behave as we have always done - that no one loves us, no one understands us, that we are basically unworthy, that the world is a dangerous place or that we have to take care of ourselves or no one will. But when we take a risk, it can be a strong wake up - shocking but also liberating to see these bubbles as just old clothes.

Combining these four healing aspects – understanding and compassion, getting a reality check from a trusted person, feeling the child inside the bubble and taking risks, we slowly begin to see the bubbles for what they are and watch as they come and go. We may still go into them but when we do, there is an awareness of what is happening and that awareness takes us out of them.

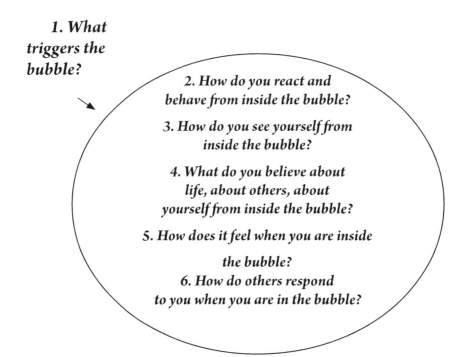

The Bubble

1. What triggers the bubble?
2. How do you react and behave from inside the bubble?
3. How do you see yourself from inside the bubble?
4. What do you believe about life, about others, about yourself from inside the bubble?
5. How does it feel when you are inside the bubble?
6. How do others respond to you when you are in the bubble?

Exercise: Identifying Our Bubbles

Pick a situation that has made you feel disturbance, pain or frustration. Can you detect that you have entered into a familiar state? We call this a bubble.

Begin to identify the characteristics of this state:

a. What provokes it? Are these triggers familiar and repetitive?
b. How does this state feel?
c. How do you feel and think about life, others and yourself when you are in it?
d. How do you react from this state and is it repetitive?

e. How do others react to you when you are in this state?
f. What do you believe to be true about others and yourself in this state - how do you see others and yourself?
g. What are your deepest fears and insecurities in this space?

Often you cannot notice that you are in a bubble until after you have come out of it. Can you notice the difference between how you feel, act and think when you are in it from how it feels afterwards (When you are in your bubble, you are taken over, and possessed by your child state of mind. Later, it is easier to observe it.)

Chapter 3:

THE MIRROR

When we are in a bubble, life responds to us in predictable ways. Different bubbles get different responses. Life and people are mirroring our "bubbleness" back to us. We could think of this process as a kind of radio transmitter sending out messages. When we are in a bubble and are strongly identified with the child inside the bubble, we are sending out a constant message that is unique to that bubble. Then we get a predictable message back. It is like looking in a mirror. When we begin to be able to see the reflection we get back and begin to understand the messages that we send out, we begin our journey out of the imprisonment of our emotional child.

Recently Amana and 1 were giving a one-day workshop outside of Zurich. Wilhelm, one of the participants, arrived a bit early and parked in a spot that was reserved for one of the residents of the seminar house. As we arrived, we noticed that he and the resident were involved in a heated exchange about whether he could park his car in that spot. When we started the workshop, during one of my initial explanations, Wilhelm raised his hand and surprised me with a vehement attack at what I was saying. Later in the day, he shared that his girlfriend had just left him and he could not understand why. He was also totally surprised that another participant in the workshop did not feel like doing an exercise with him. Wilhelm was not aware of what the mirror was reflecting back to him, nor was he aware of what he was putting out that was creating this reflection.

The Mirror Shows How We Impact Others
Most of us are not as provocative as Wilhelm or as unwilling to look at ourselves but we all have our blind spots. It is often difficult to see how our beliefs and behaviors are impacting others or how it is bringing us the reactions that we get from them. We tend to see the experiences that come to us as accidental or the other person's problem. My mother would always say to me that life is just about good luck or bad luck. When I would suggest that there might be more method to it than just luck, she didn't agree. (This is one unusual occasion when my mother was wrong.) Actually, once we begin to recognize our bubbles, it becomes clearer why things happen to us the way they do.

For years, I was in relationships with women who often seemed more like my daughter than my lover. They became dependent, regressed, and needy and I doled out rescue and care because I was so "caring and compassionate". But I got resentful; my caring and compassion went out the window, and all I wanted to do was be "free" and do my own thing. I would complain to my friends about my girlfriend being so dependent on me but I could not understand why I was repeating this pattern again and again. I could not understand what I was doing that caused this to happen especially because I thought it was the other person's fault that she was not able to stand on her own feet. I was not seeing that in my bubble, I was not open but hiding behind a parental role as a subtle and deceptive defense against my own shame and fear. Our relating patterns are great mirrors because they reveal our "bubblenesss" like nothing else.

Maria is an Italian woman in her early forties. She is puzzled because she doesn't understand why people in her life move away from her and tell her that she is not pleasant to be with. Her emotional child inside is very sad. The vibration that this child sends out is, "I want you to rescue me, to take away my sadness." But she cannot see it and every new rejection only makes her more sad and lonely.

Catherine, a German woman who has worked with us, complains that her man is not available to her. However, the demanding vibration that she puts out drives him away. She now sees that this demanding energy has always been with her and is how she tries to fill the emptiness inside.

> *In some mystical way, existence does not tolerate unconscious strategies and will create endless deprivation and disappointment for us until we go behind our strategies of control.*

Rebecca is an old and close friend. For as long as l have known her, she has complained about the men in her life not being available to her. While the relationship is going on, she feels continually deprived of love and attention and each relationship ends up with her being rejected. With each new rejection she feels that it is the first time even though she is well aware that it is a pattern. She sends out a subtle message that says, "please save me" which makes people push her away.

Our Behaviors Patterns Are Often Deeply Unconscious
Our behaviors are deeply ingrained and automatic. Sometimes we push people away with a behavior that makes them not able to trust us. Or we send out a message that says, "I don't feel loveable and I need your approval and attention to make me feel okay with myself." There was a time in my life when

women were rejecting me over and over again. I could not understand why and I was feeling very sorry for myself. I did not realize at the time that this was happening because I had not explored my wounds of shame and abandonment. I was going to women, as a beggar with the energy of a little boy wanting approval and unconditional love from a mother.

Per is a Norwegian mountain man and he is as dry as a "knekkebrød" (the Norwegian cracker bread). In a workshop he attended with us, after every session, he promptly put on his running clothes and took off for a six mile run in the countryside. He is over fifty but he doesn't have a pound of fat on his body. Per is a true loner. He was once married but he spent so much time working and engaged in all his outdoor activities that his wife left him in exasperation. He dates women but he never allows himself to get "involved". I once asked him if he had ever been in love and his answer was, "Well, I wouldn't go so far." Per only sees in the mirror someone who wants to invade him and take away his freedom. He is full of mistrust but he cannot connect his lifestyle of isolation with his deep fear of being invaded and abused. He is not asking the right questions yet.

In each of these examples, the problem arises because each person is living in his or her bubble without awareness. Furthermore, without allowing themselves to connect with the feelings underneath, their lives become run by their "bubble behavior".

Existence makes a persistent effort to show us what we need to see. It will continue to shine this mirror in our face until we see what it is saying. Normally our response in these kinds of situations is to feel angry, victimized and unjustly treated.

But all that only brings us bitterness and resignation. From this frame of mind, we are not open to seeing what we need to see about ourselves or feeling what we need to feel. Usually, we are not aware of the messages we are sending out because there is no one inside of us watching. We are living in our emotional child and acting unconsciously from this space. The feedback we often get is not what we want or expect and so we get upset and disappointed. Then we blame the feedback as not being understanding, sensitive, attentive, or loving enough. We even try to change the feedback. We can't understand why the feedback keeps coming back the same because we don't realize that we keep sending out the same message. And these reflections are not one-time events. *They are patterns.*

Christina and Alberto have been to a relationship for four years. They break up and come together again every few months. She is a beautiful 34-year-old woman who has always used her beauty and sexuality to get what she wants and has been able to manipulate men quite effectively with these two weapons. Alberto is strong enough not to get caught to her traps. But he believes that the only way to deal with her sexual demands and periodic tantrums is by cutting her off. Each time this happens, she complains bitterly that he doesn't love her and often acts out by finding another man to sleep with. Then she tires of this and comes back to him.

From his side, after a certain point, he decides that he has had enough of this relationship, in fact, of relationship in general and goes back to his familiar Zen lifestyle of isolation. Both Alberto and Christina are sending out the same message - "I don't trust you and you are not going to take advantage of me." From this bubble of mistrust, their relating becomes dominated with strategies of control and manipulation. They get lost in their automatic behavior of defending themselves from the other person.

Asking the Right Questions
We suggest that as soon as someone detects a pattern, it is helpful to start asking certain specific questions:

- The first is - "What is the reflection which people or life are giving back to me?" Or, "What is the energetic feedback I am receiving?"
- The second is - "What is the vibration which I am sending out that is causing this reflection?"
- The third is - "What is the wound which is behind this vibration?"

Just asking the question sincerely is enough. It seems to set something magical in motion as if we are asking existence to help us understand ourselves more deeply. When we start to ask these questions, we may not get an answer right away. But simply starting to ask them opens us to begin receiving the answer. Then we have taken the first step behind our automatic behavior.

From the unconsciousness of the emotional child that is framed in fear, shame and mistrust, it is hard for us to be receptive to life. From that perspective, we keep recycling the same painful patterns over and over again. *But when we have more understanding for how our emotional child thinks, feels and behaves, we can slowly begin to change our perspective.* We can begin to take what comes as opportunities to learn more about ourselves. Just shifting to this receptive space and having a willingness to look inside creates a radical change.

*"You don't see the world as it is – you see it as
Your mind forces your to see it.
Unless you are able to put the whole mind aside
And see the world differently,
Immediately with your consciousness,
You will never be able to see the truth"*
Osho

Exercise: Seeing the Reflection.
What message might existence be sending back to you from situations in your life that are painful – such as failure or rejection?

    a. Can you detect what your emotional child might be putting out which is creating this reflection?

    b. What is the wound that this pattern might be bringing up?

Part 2:
THE EMOTIONAL CHILD IN ACTION

Chapter 4:

REACTIONS AND CONTROL

In the next five chapters, we explore what we could call "bubble behavior". These are the main behavior patterns that we move into unconsciously, automatically, and compulsively when we are taken over by the emotional child state of mind. The first is *reactiveness and control*.

> *A child is naturally reactive because he or she has no space to contain fear or pain. He or she has no space to defer gratification or to tolerate frustration.*

All this makes us reactive. In this child state, when we feel someone or something threatening us in any way, we automatically move to defend or protect very rapidly. This can be a real threat but most often it is a situation into which we read threat because of our past traumas. Also, whenever we suspect that we are not going to get what we need, we react. We act first and think or feel later (sometimes all we do is react). We move from trigger to response in record time. And in between the trigger and the reaction is the whole unexplored world of our threatened, abandoned, traumatized inner self. When our energy is consumed by our automatic and habitual reactiveness, we are not able to "be with" what drives it; we don't look behind the reactions.

To our emotional child, there is an overwhelming compulsion to act because he or she feels that life depends on it. Our experiences from the past have taught us that our survival depends on whatever strategies we develop to get our needs met. In this state of unconsciousness, our only concern is to get the security or the love in whatever way possible as quickly as possible. Often we are in a reaction without any awareness that what has triggered it. The actual trigger may seem trivial and stupid but it never seems trivial to the child.

> *We may judge our reaction and feel bad about ourselves for what we did or said. We may even try to control our reactions. But neither judging nor feeling guilty nor trying to control our reactiveness has any effect on the reactivity of our wounded self. It is important to appreciate how compelling and how powerful our reactiveness is.*

Often we are not aware of the trigger until long after we have reacted, been reacted back to, reacted again and on and on. At some point, we could stop, look and ask ourselves, "Gee, seems like I have been reacting, I wonder what the trigger was?" Something has triggered our emotional child but since we are not accustomed to inquiring into our woundedness, we live from trigger to reaction quite unconsciously.

Paying Attention to What Triggers Reaction
Some years ago, Amana and I were involved in an experiment with other friends in the growth community in which we used to live. We took two weeks to investigate our reactiveness.

Each time we noticed ourselves becoming reactive, we would note it down in a little notebook that we carried around with us. We would observe what provoked the reaction and in which way we reacted. It was a beautiful window into our automatic behavior. And also, on a deeper level, into our individual wounds.

I cite a few examples of my own exploration. Feeling judged or misunderstood probably ranked as my strongest triggers. Another powerful trigger was feeling that someone had treated me with disrespect. These situations registered highest on my reaction barometer. But I also noticed that I got disturbed if I felt that someone else was getting too much attention or if they were behaving in a way which I felt was childish and entitled even if I had nothing to do with the behavior. I also noticed that anything involving the practical matters of the world such as taxes, insurance, or even making travel plans could make me irritable. I could get easily triggered if I was inconvenienced or made to wait. This could come up if someone was late for an appointment or something as trivial as a shop attendant taking a long time seeing other shoppers.

Incompetence and inefficiency was another obvious trigger for me. During my years in India, I had many opportunities to observe this particular trigger since it is always a bit of a surprise when something in India works and if it does, one never knows for how long. I could be provoked in situations where I am out of control such as sitting in the passenger seat of a car or feeling that someone has power over me. I also hate it when something mechanical doesn't work. In all of these situations, it is the feelings of helplessness that I hate.

In any given day, if we are paying attention, we probably can discover many triggers that can provoke a reaction. The list is long but there does seem to be some common themes:

1. *Threat* – feeling attacked, invaded, interfered with, criticized, and judged.
2. *Hurt* – feeling unappreciated, not considered or rejected.
3. *Expectations* – feeling someone's demands or expectations.
4. *Reflections* – seeing some quality in another that you don't accept in yourself.
5. *Comparison* – comparing ourselves unfavorably with another.
6. *Fear of loss* of someone or something.
7. Being *inconvenienced or uncomfortable*.

Paying Attention to Our Reactions
Once triggered, we react in many different ways. How we react depends much on our emotional nature. Some of us are extroverted and fiery while others of us are more introverted and withdrawn. When I feel hurt, I often pull inside. I may even pretend that nothing has bothered me. I may not even *know* that something has disturbed me. I find that Karen Horney's (see references) categories of how people react is brilliant. She observed that people react by moving against people, moving toward people, or moving away from people.

Different Kinds of Reactions
1. The moving-out reactions – *demanding, blaming, attacking, rebelling, taking revenge, being angry and irritable, criticizing, judging and complaining.*

2. The moving-toward reactions – *harmonizing, rescuing, begging, pleasing.*
3. The moving-away reactions – *withdrawing, pouting and brooding, collapsing, becoming depressed and giving up or resigning.*

We each have our own reactive style that can be a unique mix of all three. And often, we react differently with different people. We might move away from or toward someone we fear and move against someone with whom we feel more empowered.

How we react also depends on the emotional environment of our childhood and how we witnessed our parents, especially our same sex parent, react. In my childhood, there was little or no overt expression of emotion. I never saw my father cry and rarely did I see him show anger. He kept his anger inside and would show it with irritability and impatience. That was my imprinting. My emotional style is much like my father's. For a long time, I fought it until I finally accepted that this is how my emotional child is and I found it a relief to accept my reactive style whatever it is.

Finally, our reactions are deeply influenced by our cultural conditioning. We lead workshops in many different countries and we have become used to how different the temperament is depending on whether we are working with Americans, Scandinavians, Germans, Swiss, Italians, Turks, Russians, Chinese or French Canadians.

Strategies of Control

Control is actually another type of reaction of our emotional child but it can appear deceptively adult-like and sophisticated. Most of us are "control-freaks" in one way or another. It is just too dangerous for our child to feel that he or she has no control over things. Our control strategies are creative and subtle. We manipulate, overpower, threaten, seduce, convince, deceive, guilt, rescue, and give advice – a plethora of highly unconscious methods of feeling secure which we have cultivated since early childhood.

We can control by become addicted to power or money. We can structure our lives and our behavior to such an extent that all spontaneity vanishes from our life. And all of these are nothing more than our emotional child devoid of trust and afraid of letting go. We can observe our controlling behavior in many aspects of our life – in relating, money, work, eating, making love, even driving the car.

When I was young, I had two aunts who lived in New York and when we visited from Europe where we lived, we would spend time visiting both. In one home, I never felt comfortable. Everything seemed uptight and obsessively clean and I was always afraid of making a mistake (which I invariably did). In the other, even though she lived in a much poorer section of town, I felt totally at home the moment I arrived.

Now I realize that the way that these two aunts related to the fears of their emotional child was totally different. The first could not face them and had attempted to build a lifestyle of control to prevent herself from feeling them. The second was intuitively and consciously in touch with her frightened child. Even though it wasn't until much later that I began to consciously work with my wounded self, I could already tell that this aunt had wisdom. She became a kind of mentor for me. When I went to college my parents were living in Israel and she was the one I often turned to when I needed support. Even though, (perhaps because) she had suffered greatly in her life, she emanated a rare trust in life.

We can apply the same kind of awareness to our control strategies as we do with our reactions. Reaction has a definite kinesthetic (inner body) feel to it. So does control. I notice that when Amana is driving, I move automatically into a controlling space and begin making comments about her performance. Even when I don't say anything, I am thinking them. I can feel my frightened child behind this behavior. I also begin to feel my control when I am giving advice (which I *used* to do often) or when I am judging others (which I have been known to do once or twice). I also recognize and feel the control behind my overworking and staying busy.

Behind the Reaction is a Frightened Child
When I could understand more deeply where all this behavior was coming from inside of me it became much easier to accept it. I have judged my reactiveness and control. But I can see that it is a primitive effort to control and master my environment so that I won't feel frightened, hurt or invaded.

> *When we were traumatized as a child either in our home or at school, we were not able to respond appropriately. As a result, we lost confidence in our ability to master our environment.*

Our reactions and control strategies are our wounded self's way of learning to master what he or she never mastered earlier. Unfortunately, this behavior does not accomplish what it is intended to accomplish. It doesn't make us more centered and more confident. We cannot achieve greater centeredness and self-confidence when we are involved in behavior that comes from the emotional child state of mind. It cannot bring us the sense of mastery we seek because in this state of unconsciousness, we are fear-based. To gain the mastery and centeredness we seek, we have to learn to respond to our environment from another place in our consciousness - from our meditativeness and clarity.

You are moving in the market,
Doing your work, coming back home,
Fighting, loving, hating, eating, sleeping
Doing all sorts of things –
But the whole thing is happening as if you are a robot.
Watch any mood.
Is there a gap between the insult and the reaction?
Is there a gap when you meditate?
Osho

Exercise: Observing Disturbance and Reactions

a. Notice in a day each time you feel disturbed for any reason. Ask yourself, "What caused me to feel disturbed?" "What specifically did someone say or not say, do or not do, which created this disturbance?" Or if it was not a person who caused the disturbance, ask yourself, "what situation and what was it specifically about the situation which caused my disturbance?"

b. Then, notice how you reacted to this disturbance. What did you do or not do? How did you try to change the situation or the person? How did you try to change yourself?

c. Notice the response that the reaction creates in the other person. Is it anger, distance, fight, shock or pleasing.

How does this response feel to you? Are you getting what you wanted from the other person?

d. Finally, consider the wounds that underlie the reaction? In what way did it make you feel rejected, shamed, frightened, frozen, overwhelmed, mistrustful or controlled?

e. Notice if this trigger/reaction mechanism is new or familiar and if you have repeated it in the past. You may even be able to trace this back to your childhood.

Chapter 5:

EXPECTATIONS AND ENTITLEMENT

The second behavior style of our emotional child is expectations and entitlement. We all expect. And much of the time, we believe that our expectations are totally reasonable. We have found that this is the most challenging behavior pattern to bring into awareness. We cling to our expectations like stubborn mules because on the other side of expectations is disappointment, pain, and aloneness.

> *It is a painful awakening to let go of expectations. It means waking up to a world that is not how our emotional child would like it to be.*

I always covered up my expectations with denial. But once I began to see them, I have been amazed at how much of my life is colored in expectations. I have expectations about how people treat me, how much and in what way they love me, how my creativity is appreciated, how prompt and responsible people are in giving me what I want, and in anticipating my feelings and moods. I have great expectations about being understood and even about the weather. When I didn't get my expectations met, I reacted. Sometimes I blamed, sometimes I pretended I didn't care. Sometimes I got irritable. Mostly I wasn't even been aware that I had an expectation until it wasn't met and found myself irritated without knowing why. The reason was always the same. Something was not happening the way I wanted it to.

It never occurred to me that all this was just the emotional child inside. But once I began to understand about this buried part of me and the state of consciousness that goes with it, it became clear. The reactions have become less and less frequent and when they occur, I can catch them quickly. We are often asked in our workshops, if there is life after expectation or if there is any point being in a relationship if we don't expect. It is definitely a different way to live.

Expectation Are Driven By Fear
It is natural that our child inside expects. It is a deep survival mechanism. Our expectations are driven by fear. We are afraid that we will not get what we need or will be hurt in some way and on the deepest level that we will cease to exist. This creates an almost unbearable sense of panic. In our child state of mind, we must turn to our outside environment to get what we lack because in the mind of a child, we know no other way to get our essential needs met.

Unfortunately, we don't usually realize that this panicked child is driving our actions. This behavior creates problems in our lives because expectations result in frustration and disappointment. No one ever changes to fulfill our expectations - even if they try. Furthermore, it creates resentment and drives people away from us.

> *A life built around expectations results in endless disappointment, rejection, frustration, low self-esteem, and even*

self-destruction. Expectations are an attempt to find something on the outside that can only be found inside. Our expectations are an attempt to fill our holes, our inner feelings of emptiness, from the outside.

For instance, we attempt to fill our abandonment fears by expecting that people be there for us. We attempt to fill our fears of invasion by expecting people to respect our boundaries. When we expect something from someone, no matter how reasonable it may seem, we are still not seeing that person at that moment for who he or she is. We are hoping or demanding that the person be how we want him or her to be. In our child state of mind we are not able to allow the other person to be as he or she is because we are not able to be with the feelings of betrayal and abandonment that come when others don't meet our expectations. Behind every expectation is a wound or a hole but we are seldom aware that it is there or what it is. When someone does not meet our expectations, we are disturbed because we feel the wound of betrayal, invasion or abandonment inside.

I have a friend who has not been very responsible or accountable. I have been through all kinds of agony because, for a long time, I expected him to be as I wanted him to be and I felt so justified in having these expectations. The way he behaved was not listed in my inner dictionary definition of "good friendship". When my expectations were unmet, I would react with anything from rage to resignation and despair. I focused on my disappointment rather than on how this was provoking deep feelings of betrayal.

Once I started to stay with my own feelings, I was no longer so compelled to react automatically. I began to see and accept him as he is. Not from resignation but from clarity. And from this clarity, I realized that I needed to change the nature of our relationship so that I was no longer trapped into expecting. If we made a plan to meet, I wouldn't count on his meeting that commitment. The behavior that made me feel so betrayed in the past stopped bothering me.

Entitlement Are Expectations In Disguise
One important aspect of expectation is the energy of entitlement. This is the attitude of "I deserve!" "You owe it to me!" It goes hand in hand with expectations. Sometimes our entitlement is out in the open. We actually believe that the other person or the situation owes us attention or whatever else we expect and we feel indignant and outraged when we don't get it.

For example, I have a friend who has always expected that people, particularly his lover, should be relaxed, centered, and loving around him. When they aren't, he has felt invaded and disturbed and gets angry. He would get disturbed because he felt that when someone close to him is tense or angry, he couldn't relax. He would blame and complain whenever this happened. But over the years, he has seen that this is just "his stuff". In the moments that he feels disturbed, he has the choice to go in and feel his disturbance rather than react on whatever or whoever is causing it.

> *Our entitlement is deep and unconscious. We get irritated and may even throw a tantrum when things don't go our way but often we can't actually verbalize why we are so upset.*

Another indication of our entitlement is that we do things that indicate that we expect things but we are unconscious why we are doing them or even that we are doing them. For instance, we leave little messes around with the expectation that someone will clean up after us. Or we make people wait because we unconsciously expect others to be at our beck and call. In our entitlement, we just don't consider other peoples' feeling. After twenty years of working with myself, I am still surprised at how entitled I can be sometimes especially about the smallest things.

> *We are entitled because we are terrified to let go of control and just allow life and people to be as it is. In our child frame of mind, we associate letting go with harm and deprivation of love.*

We grow up feeling empty inside but also with a conditioning that the only way to get what you need is to demand it. This creates a double agony. We are feeling deprived and desperate but when we make an effort to get what we need, we don't get what we want. And deep inside, we don't like ourselves for being so demanding or reactive. Yet in our child state of mind, we don't know any other way. Also, we are seldom aware of all the little ways that our entitlement shows itself. This attitude (and all the behaviors that come from it) is so deeply buried in our psyche that even if someone points it, we may have no idea what he or she are talking about.

When the adult mind attaches to our entitlement, we can get very righteous about the things we expect. "After all," we say, "people should treat each other fairly and with consideration." "Of course I expect that this person should be fair and kind, don't you?" Or "This is how the other person should behave if he or she says he loves me. What is love about anyway?" And so on. All our personal standards support and fuel our entitlement and our expectations. These standards come from our emotional child attempting to create order and harmony. Life is as it is, people are how they are, and it has nothing to do with our standards.

But our emotional child is not interested in such truths. Our expectations are deep. Some of them we may be aware of, others we cover with denial. I hid mine behind all kinds of fancy spiritual ideas pretending that I was beyond this or not needing that. But our intimate relationships can be very effective at uncovering them - sooner or later. Unknowingly, we approach our current relationships full of entitlement. It may take a little time for them to surface, but they always do.

For example, anti-dependents (those who tend to avoid intimacy) expect the other to be sensitive and respectful of their needs and feelings and give them plenty of "space". Dependents (those who tend to crave intimacy) expect that the other person will be there for them and give them plenty of "love and attention". We can look at any area of our life with our partners, such as sex, money, communication, or cleanliness and notice that it is full of expectations.

Our Expectations Reflect Our Past Betrayals
Our expectations accurately reflect the ways that we have felt betrayed or invaded in the past. We expect that people will not treat us in a way that triggers these wounds. When someone triggers one of my wounds. I get upset. For instance, because I was invaded with advice and being patronized as a child, I

have gotten livid when I felt someone close of me was doing this. I am expecting that they should not treat me this way.

It is totally reasonable to expect people to do what they say they are going to do. It is also totally reasonable to expect people to treat us with respect. But often they don't. Our expectations only frustrate us and bring us pain. They certainly don't change the way other people think or behave. When we hold on to the belief that our expectations are reasonable and that people, whomever they are, should live up to our expectations, we are not able to penetrate behind them. We are not able to see what our expectation is covering. And then we are not able to see and feel our wounds that get triggered when the expectation is not met. We just feel righteous and victimized. And even more importantly, we are not able to see the person for who he or she is.

Examining our expectations is a powerful way to explore our wounds of being betrayed or invaded. We don't even have to dig around in our past because we are getting triggered right in the here and now. We attract situations that bring up precisely the ways in which these traumas happened in the past and get re-enacted in the present. It comes up with our lover, children, employers, teachers, parents (of course) and friends. When we feel disappointed or frustrated, behind that feeling is the expectation.

Behind the expectation is the wound.

For instance, I hate it when I am made to wait. I expect that people will be on time. Behind this is my wound of not feeling recognized. It makes me feel insignificant and I am right back to that younger brother who felt second. When I take the time to go through this little meditation, it brings much more space inside. Rather than live life in frustration and disappointment, I can go inside. Not that I don't get angry or upset.

> *But normally we stop there. We live with our entitlement and feel justified in having it. We live unconsciously in an emotional child frame of mind looking at the world through eyes of expectations and then being continually frustrated when people or the world disappoint us. Going back from the anger to the expectation to the wound adds much more dimension.*

The Expectation Meditation
Noticing the frustration
Tracing back to the expectation
Feeling the wound

Negative Expectations

Sometimes, we want something but are so afraid of not getting it that we just expect the opposite. It is as though our collapse is sitting on our expectations and holding them back. The safest way to prevent feeling disappointment or frustration for not having our expectations met is simply to deny them. I call this "the parking space syndrome". When I was young, we lived in Paris for many years. Whenever we went to the movies, my mother would often say that we couldn't go because we would never find a space to park. If I could convince her to go, we would often grab the first parking space we found even if it was right close to our house because she insisted that we would never find any other space closer. Then we would have to walk a long way or even take the subway to get to the theatre. When we got there, invariably, we would notice a parking spot close-by.

When we minimize our needs, it may actually seem that we don't have expectations – but we do. I have found that my irritability is one of the best ways to smoke out those expectations that I have denied or minimized. For instance, I can get irritable if a workshop doesn't fill. If I go behind the irritability, there is the expectation that *all our workshops should fill*. And behind that is the fear that we are no longer in demand and the insecurity that I am not good at what I do. Often, I may be too proud to admit it, but it helps to know that it is just my emotional child in operation.

It is pointless to focus only on changing our reactive behavior patterns. Unless we tap into the fear and insecurity that is driving them, no fundamental transformation happens. If we have an addictive or abusive pattern, it *is* important to use some discipline to stop these behaviors because otherwise our life will suffer greatly. But ultimately, the work involves dealing with what is underneath.

It is also pointless to try and stop expecting. Our child inside expects. That is just how he or she is and will always be. It is a big part of our emotional child. We can transcend expectation by noticing it and going deeper inside to explore the fears and insecurities that lie behind them. Then they start to drop away by themselves. We transcend expectations by maturing into seeing people and things as they are, not as we would like them to be.

> *"A men of consciousness has no*
> *expectations,*
> *Hence he is never frustrated"*
> Osho

Exercises:
1. Exploring Entitlement:

Allow yourself to tune into the energy inside of feeling that people, a person, or life in general owes something to you. Allow yourself to feel this energy in the body. Notice how this energy shows itself in your life.

2. Exploring Expectations:

Considering your most significant relationships, what are your greatest expectations?

1. I expect that the person be present and available for me.
2. I expect that the person is considerate and listens to me.
3. I expect that the person is sensitive to my limits perhaps even without my having to say anything.
4. I expect that the person provides for me financially.
5. I expect that the person touches me sensitively.
6. I expect that the person doesn't control or manipulate me for his or her own needs and wants.
7. I expect that the person is in his or her energy and not collapsed or wishy-washy.
8. I expect that the person does not expect me to rescue him or her.
9. I expect that the person works on him or herself and is not in a state of denial about his feelings.

10. I expect that the person is meditative and conscious in how he or she lives (living space, care of the body etc.).
11. I expect that the person is sensitive and supportive of my creativity and spiritual growth.

3. Exploring Your Reactions to Unmet Expectations:

For each unfulfilled expectation, notice your reaction. Is it anger, demand, blame, withdrawal, resignation, denying or minimizing that you care?

Notice what comes up when you take your attention away from the other person and just feel how it is not have this expectation met?

4. Exploring Expectations in Different Areas of Your Life

For a closer exploration of your unconscious expectations, look at the various areas of your life. What are your expectations connected to sexuality, feelings, spirituality and growth, living together, cleanliness, money, and relating? You can also bring light to your expectations in these areas by looking at the last time you felt angry or disappointed with someone.

Chapter 6:

COMPROMISE

In a group recently, a participant shared that he had been in a relationship for seven years. Two years into it, he realized that it was not the right situation for him. But he felt trapped. He did not have the heart to tell his partner that he wanted to leave her because he was afraid of hurting her. Finally, he told her that he was gay which was not true but at least it gave him an excuse to leave without feeling so much guilt.

We will go to great extremes to compromise our integrity because our emotional child is terrified to live his or her truth. In the child state of mind, we live for others. When our consciousness is taken over by fear and shame, we cannot avoid living in compromise. Our emotional child believes that other people control our well-being. If we hold this belief, then our actions will be directed not according to our own light but toward how others think and behave.

Our Emotional Child Focuses on Approval

In the emotional child state of mind, most of our focus is directed toward getting love, approval, attention, and respect. We may pretend that we do not need or want all this but it is usually a denial. We feed on attention and approval because we were starved of it. We are in a continuous struggle to get what we lack. One of the main ways that we attempt to get this attention, love, approval, and respect is by adapting ourselves. Our life becomes an endless string of compromises. Furthermore, our emotional child is terrified of even the slightest disapproval or of being physically or verbally attacked in any way. *He or she is a harmony junkie.* When faced with having to confront anyone, we can get overwhelmed in fear. It is safer to compromise.

Compromise, like all the other behaviors of our emotional child, is automatic. For instance, when someone you respect, and whose friendship and attention you want, asks you how you think about something, your child inside will automatically say what you think he or she wants to hear. When someone you fear asks you do to something, your frightened child will probably do it even if it is the last thing you want to do. The emotional child does not have the tools to do otherwise. When faced with a situation where we want something from someone, we may have already compromised before the situation even arises.

Many of us are like a dog that rolls over on his belly in submission. Situations with authority figures have been particularly poignant in my own life where the fear of disapproval and the hunger for respect drove me away from my own center. It would be more precise to say that I never even connected with my center or my integrity in these situations because the fear was so great. My whole manner was a compromise of my being. Whatever I said or did came out of that space. As I began to work with it, I became more aware of how it felt inside and connecting with the fears inside helped to understand rather than judge it.

Our intimate relating is a major area where most of us compromise endlessly - until we develop deeper understanding for our emotional child. We do not want to cause displeasure or disharmony and will go to great lengths to avoid it. For instance, a couple I have known for a long time came to our workshop for couples. In this seminar, one of the topics we deal with is the way that people who have been living together for sometime have made compromises that are creating resentment between them.

We suspected that if they did this process together, it could bring up much disharmony because the life they were living together was full of compromise. He felt he needed to play out adolescent fantasies with other women and was feeling resentful that he was so "married". She was bending over backwards to please him because she was feeling so insecure and unloved. Halfway into the workshop, he started sleeping with another woman. She reacted at first with collapse and begging, then with rage and finally began to see that she was in a pattern of pleasing daddy and needed to reclaim her dignity.

Bringing the situation out into the open and identifying how each one was living in compromise helped them to do what they felt they needed to do. He had the affair and she went on a journey to India. After four months, they came back together in a much clearer and authentic way. Before, both of them were reacting from their unconscious emotional child. In this state, anger, disapproval, or rejection from the other can create pure terror inside.

> *If we can begin to feel the fear behind the compromise, we bring awareness to how deeply this behavior rules our life. Then we have the power to choose another way to live.*

In a session that I did not long ago, a man came with much pain and confusion related to his love life. The woman, with whom he had been for six years and had a child with, had fallen in love with another man. Two weeks prior to this affair, she had told him that she wanted to have another child, buy a house, and get married. The affair had lasted only three weeks, but during this time he went through utter hell. Now they were back together again. She claimed that she was finished with the other man and now wanted to go back to their plan to buy a house, get married, and have another child.

This person is a child psychiatrist. He is over six feet two inches tall and has a very strong, attractive and imposing presence. Yet with this woman, he lives in compromise. He is terrified to do anything that she might disapprove of. He felt that if he said no to her in any way, it meant that he did not love her unconditionally. In his domestic life, he is totally "out of control". It is a though he has allowed his woman friend to drive his life and he feels helpless to do anything about it.

> *One of the lessons that many of us need to learn is how to take back the responsibility of our life at whatever the price. But in our child state of mind, this is not possible. It is too frightening.*

I faced a situation in my own relationship when Amana and I first got together that brought this issue up clearly for me. I had a close woman friend whose relationship with me was causing some difficulties and conflict between Amana and I. She is much like a sister to me and we have known each other a long time. But our relationship was dysfunctional.

She leaned on me for emotional support and was not so respectful of Amana's boundaries or mine. The difficulties came mostly because I was unclear and indirect with both women and that unclarity was making the boundaries of each relationship murky. I was dealing with the situation much as I had dealt with most situations in the past that was producing conflict. I simply stuck my head in the sand and pretended there was nothing to deal with hoping that by ignoring the issues, they would magically get better. Once I could see what I was doing and where it was all coming from, I was able to see that this was an old and familiar pattern. I could affirm both relationships and be clear with both women where I was. The conflict vanished.

Digging Into the Roots of Compromise
The roots of our compromise are more complex than just the fear of rejection, disapproval or attack. As a child, most of us formed unconscious contracts with our caretakers. In exchange for love and approval, we agreed to behave in the way that was required of us. For each of us, the kind of contract we formed is different but they all have certain life negative characteristics in common. We agreed to compromise our life energy and our nature in some way to meet the expectations of society, parents, and teachers. For this reason, this phenomenon has been called, "negative bonding". Our bonding to our caretakers came with a price. Of course, this happened so early and it was so supported by every environment that we were in that we have no idea that it happened or how it happened.

We have a Norwegian client who was raised in the upper crust of Oslo society. He was groomed to succeed in business as his father had done and, as was expected of him, he married a wealthy woman who could support his rise in importance and stature. It was a marriage built mostly on form. We first met him when he came to a training we were running. I recognized his sweetness and innocence and could feel the struggle that he was going through living up to all the standards set for him. As he went deeper in his personal growth, he found it more and more difficult to keep up the old life and he even found that he was sabotaging himself over and over again.

He eventually divorced his wife but he is still struggling to make it in the business world in Norway. It is just too frightening for him to break the negative contract that he made with his father and face his disapproval. He has brought his father's and his society's values so deeply inside that he has not yet been able to get a second divorce - the one from his negative bonding. He recently met a woman who really sees and loves him but she is so different from what he has been used to that he is afraid to present her to his old friends and family for fear of their disapproval.

The greatest difficulty with this kind of compromise is that it is so deeply ingrained inside. We may not realize we are compromising. Yet, at the same time, somewhere deep inside, something doesn't feel right. When we take on a role early in life, there may often only be a small inner whisper that reminds us that we are living in compromise.

`Many of us were conditioned to be caretakers. That's how we earned love as a child and that is what we believe earns it for us today. We may have been conditioned, as I was, to perform, so we focus all our energy in this direction at the expense of the more feminine aspects of our being.

Our Self-Image is Based in Compromise

Many of us have lived in compromise for so long that we don't know what it would be like to live otherwise. We have a self-image based on compromise. I know that I did. I remember in college, we all used to go to Humphrey Bogart movies during exam time. It was a ritual that the night before each exam, we went to see one of his movies. We figured that if we didn't know the material by then, it was too late anyway. We knew Bogart's lines so well that we all would say them out loud in the theater even before he said them. We memorized them because they were so cool, together, and uncompromising.

After each movie, I would make an inner resolution that now I was going to be that cool a guy. I even thought of buying on of those hats Bogart used to wear. It never worked. It seemed like at the first opportunity I was back into my old compromising self.

> *When we live in compromise, we feel "out of control" at a deep core place inside. There is a certain inner feeling connected to compromise.*

For me, it feels soft and ungrounded. As I became more familiar with this feeling, it helped me to recognize when I did or said something that did not feel right. I began to become very familiar with the inner feeling of compromise. At first I detected it days after. (Sometimes weeks afterwards.) Slowly the gap time shortened until I could sense it almost immediately. This was a first step to moving out of so much of my automatic behavior that was based on an old and familiar way of behaving and seeing myself as a person who compromised.

When all we have done in our life is live in compromise, we don't have much of a standard to judge when we live in dignity. Compromise filled my life and it became easy to see that this was especially true with anyone who had some kind of power over me - the power to reject, to withhold love, to affect our survival, or the power of respect. With these people, I entered into contracts to keep things harmonious but often less than alive. But even more than these situations, I began to see that my whole way of living was a compromise. I basically lived for others, not for myself.

In many ways, this has changed. Over the years, I made choices and decisions that have brought back dignity and I learned what it feels like inside to live with dignity. Once I could feel this, it was not so easy to go back to the old way again. Of course there are many times and situations when I catch myself back in the old self but less and less. The important thing is that I can tell the difference. Because learning this knack has made such a difference in my own life, it has become one of the areas that we focus on in depth in our work.

When we speak about compromise, we are referring to essential aspects of our being, not the minor accommodation that we all have to make to live harmoniously with others. For instance when I like the house to be at 68 degrees and Amana would prefer it to be 72, it is not a compromise to set it at 70. The compromising we are talking about involves essential aspects of our being and life energy - it involves doing and saying what is false to our nature and minimizing or denying essential needs and wants.

Also, coming out of compromise never means that someone else has to change. It is not about the other person, it is about our finding the courage to be who we are. That is not something that we can achieve in the child state of mind. The fear is too great. To live without compromising, we have to understand how and in which situations we do it and then begin to see that we do not have to be run by our frightened, insecure child.

> *"Remember never to compromise*
> *As far as the essential is concerned,*
> *beware.*
> *Even if you have to risk your life,*
> *Risk it."*
> Osho

Exercises:
1. Feeling the inner quality of compromise.
    a. Practice learning how it feels inside when you compromise.
    b. Notice the next time you do or say something which doesn't feel right.
    c. Notice the body sensations, how you feel about yourself, and the thoughts that arise about yourself.

2. Noticing people in your life with whom you compromise.
    a. Observe how you behave with the significant people in your life – your lover, your boss, your closest friends.
    b. Ask yourself if there is some way that they have power over you.
    c. Then notice if you compromise what you say or do around them.

3. Noticing the ways that you compromise.

Begin becoming aware of the exact ways that you compromise.
- a. Do you say what you don't mean or feel or not say what you feel?
- b. How do you behave in ways that feel false?
- c. What sorts of activities do you not do in your life because you are afraid of what another will say or do?

4. Becoming aware of the negative contracts from the past.
- a. Write down how you made contracts with your primary caretakers that earned you love and approval but compromised your life energy.
- b. What was expected of you and what did you give up?

Chapter 7:

ADDICTIVENESS

In our emotional child state of mind, we are in perpetual anxiety. We often feel helpless to deal with life's problems, overwhelmed and out of control. Often we feel in deep and intolerable shame and insecurity sometimes perpetually but particularly when provoked by failure or rejection. Sometimes these feelings are greater and sometimes less but they are always there. The child cannot contain this anxiety. He or she wants some relief from this unbearable anxiety and feelings of helplessness and turns to anything that can somehow ease the pain. This is the basis of addictive behavior. When the fears and pain of these wounds are triggered, we become even more addiction prone.

> *The pull toward addiction comes from our child state of consciousness. In our child state, we have little ability to contain frustration, anxiety and to control impulses.*

This part of us lacks the perspective to suffer through difficult times with a vision toward long-range goals and general well-being. When I attended the "Lifespring Trainings" years ago (human potential courses that were popular in the seventies and eighties), they taught that life is about "short range pain for long range pleasure". That concept is impossible for our emotional child.

While I realized that this is a major behavior pattern of our emotional child, I had difficulty finding out what I wanted to write in this chapter. My difficulties with compulsive and self-destructive behavior have been minimal in my life compared to others I know. Perhaps that is because in spite of other difficulties I had in my childhood and adolescence, I was given the gift of a lot of love and structure. My parents provided a very secure holding environment for a child, with much security, support and inspiration to learn, and to appreciate life. There was never any fear of survival and the priorities that I was given were clear – I was taught that constant learning, living responsibly, and finding meaning by helping others is what matters in life. Not only did they stress education, they also paid for it – an expensive college education and medical school. And there was never any question that they would pay; they simply saw that as good parenting. I took this so for granted that it was not until much later that I was able to feel the gratitude.

Later, after college, during the period of my life when I was without direction, struggling to find my own way in life and often feeling depressed and aimless, even then, I never got lost in self-destructive behavior. I experimented with a few drugs during that time but mostly they were psychedelics and I did them with a clear intention that they were part of a deep inner spiritual search. During that time, I had two experiences that changed my life.

The first happened while I was spending a year in law school. I knew that this career was not for me but I had no idea what was. I spent many hours alone in my room just lying on my bed and looking up at the ceiling. Many days, it felt like I was lost in a dark hole and on one day, in particular, I felt that I was falling deeper and deeper into this hole, until all of a sudden, I stopped and I had the sensation that I was being held in some mystical way. I had the clear feeling that no matter how far I could fall, I would always reach this place of being held. Shortly after that experience, I knew that I would not return to law school and that what I needed was a lot of time living without the thought of career or future. I moved to California and spent several years as a "hippie drop out".

The second experience happened during those "drop out" years. I was with some friends at the Grand Canyon and decided to take LSD. This was a time when periodically, I would do LSD or "magic mushrooms". But this time was different. Walking alone into the Canyon, I felt like I was seeing God everywhere I looked. And after going through intense fear that I would die, I imagined that I heard a voice inside my head saying, "You have received everything that you will ever receive from taking psychedelic drugs. Now it is time to find a spiritual master." I didn't even know what a spiritual master was then but some years later; I was on my way to India to do precisely that. And I never did any more drugs after that day. I suspect that the reason I never got lost either in depression or substance abuse is largely because of the foundation I got as a child.

There are Many Ways to Be Addicted
In our work, we are faced with people all the time who are grappling with one form of addiction or another. Neither of us have addiction prone personalities so we have had to learn second hand - from close friends and clients who have struggled to overcome troublesome addictions of different

kinds such as compulsive marijuana or cigarette smoking, alcohol, pornography, or compulsive sexuality. We are humbled by what these people have gone through and always deeply touched when they are able to stay in recovery.

Still, on a deep level, we all have a part of us that seeks to run away from fear and pain. There are many ways of running away – entertainment, shopping, eating, socializing, isolating, sports, even meditating. If we want to run away, we will find a way to do it, that is the basis of addiction.

> *Behind our addictiveness, as with the other behaviors of the emotional child, is fear and shame and an unwillingness to be with that fear and shame. When stress arises, the child in us automatically reaches for some source of instant gratification.*

When I have been able to look inside in those moments when I see myself obsessively and robotically numbing myself, I can feel the franticness and the shame. My way of dealing with frustration has largely been to compensate for it with activity, discipline, and control. That, I have discovered, is also a kind of addiction because it is driven by the same inner forces that run all addictive behavior – by the compulsion to avoid feeling fear and shame. For a long time, I judged myself and anyone else whom I felt was addictive or self-indulgent.

I inherited this attitude from my father. His motivation, drive, and self-control were so strong that it intimidated most people who knew him. He disciplined himself to such an extent that the only time I remember ever seeing him doing anything self-indulgent was when he ate ice cream or smelly French cheeses which he loved. He taught himself seven foreign languages and learned to play three musical instruments so well that he played in orchestras and in chamber groups until shortly before he died. My mother also has always been very self-sacrificing.

Raised in this frame and following in the footsteps of an older brother whose drive and motivation were as strong as my father's, I learned to be strongly self-motivated but also to become driven, judgmental, and harsh on myself or others. I have allowed myself few lapses in self-control. In short, I covered my addictiveness with control in the same way that my father and brother did. I saw people as either on course or indulgent and there was little in between.

It is not hard to imagine that in this environment, there was not much room for me to feel my vulnerability - or anyone else's for that matter. Slowly, through a psychiatric residency and years in therapy, much of this harshness began to chip away. On one of the first days after I had arrived in India and was at the ashram, listening to my master speaking, he said something that changed my life. "Discipline," he said, "only strengthens the ego."

It All Comes Down to Control or Indulgence
Addictiveness is different for each of us and it comes in many forms. But basically, the emotional child deals with frustration and anxiety in one of two ways – with extreme and compulsive self or external control or self-indulgence. To ease the tension and constant anxiety that is always inside, we move to one of these two extremes. I have observed that some people who are recovering from an addiction will go from the extreme of indulgence to control and fanaticism (what they

call a "dry drunk"). It is still addiction, less self-destructive to be sure, but not home.

Each one of us has to find own way to heal addiction. I am aware of all the controversy in the addiction field about whether or not it is a disease with genetic roots, whether or not it is a lifelong affliction, if a former addict must attend 12-step support meetings forever and finally, if an addict can ever touch again whatever substance he or she has been addicted to. I have close friends and many clients who have been through recovery of one form or another and they have vehemently supported both sides of this controversy. For some, the twelve-step support system and philosophy works well. For others, it doesn't and they have to find another source of support and guidance.

But one thing that we have definitely learned, no one recovers from an addiction until he or she feels that the pain of continuing is worse than the pain of stopping and the pleasure of stopping is greater than the pleasure of continuing. That decision cannot come from our emotional child. It comes from our mature state of consciousness, from our higher wisdom. It is our emotional child that drives us to addiction because it has little or no space to deal with frustration, disappointment, pain, or fear. We heal addiction by knowing when and how we are in the grips of this part of us and by finding the resources to feel and contain the anxiety, fear and shame that lie underneath our addictiveness.

Perhaps if we were raised in environments that were relaxed, not pressured, supportive and immensely loving, we wouldn't be so addiction-prone. But when I began to appreciate the amount of stress that our vulnerability and sensitivity has been subjected to, it makes sense that we would naturally reach for something which could lessen the inner tension.

Clarity of Intention and Inner Space

There are countless sources of stress descending on our vulnerability, all of which creates anxiety and causes us to crave relief. One is the constant struggle to prove ourselves to others and to ourselves. Because we may have covered our shame so automatically and unknowingly, it is often hard to appreciate how much stress we put ourselves under all the time. All the pressure that comes from our culture to succeed and be "somebody" puts our inner sensitivity into deep shame and shock. To keep up with this fast, materialistic, achievement oriented world, we have to live in denial of our sensitivity. The insanity of Western culture often runs our lives. And then there are our deep fears of feeling the loneliness and emptiness inside.

Even though our emotional child has no resources for dealing with this dark hole of loneliness and meaninglessness, we can find the resources now as an adult. One such resource is discovering a reason to feel what we have been running away from. Before we can stop an addictive pattern, we have to feel a strong motivation to do so. Our intention has to be crystal clear. We have to recognize how it is affecting our life, our state of consciousness and our feeling connected to ourselves, our body, others and life itself. We have to become acutely aware of the price we are paying.

Then, we have to feel and know intuitively that we are ready and have the inner space to face the fear and shame that we have been avoiding. Finding inner space to deal with pain and fear is a bit like building inner muscle. Each time we take a small step toward hanging in there with the discomfort and even terror, we learn that we can do it. We also discover that it passes.

A client of ours has spent many years as a heroin addict and only came to work with us when he realized that he was killing himself. In the course of three years, he attended our seminars and our training, following us to different countries to complete our full curriculum. In that time period, his transformation was astonishing. From being isolated, aggressive, and belligerent, especially with women, he began to feel and expose his vulnerability more and more frequently. From blaming others for his pain, now he regularly owns his own fears and reveals them. He wants to become a teacher of our work and we have supported him to train as a certified teacher. It is always a mystery why one person has the ability to recover and another does not. In his case, I suspect that it was his intelligence and his passion for life that carried him through.

> *Containing fear and pain is both a mindset that "I have the inner space to hold the discomfort and let it be as it is" and it is also an inner knowing that we have the strength to do it.*

We have also found that the more sensitive and vulnerable we become, our addictive tendencies can become worse. As we get more in touch with the fears and pain inside, the anxieties that we have suppressed with denial and control rise to the surface.

One of my deepest investigations in myself has been to find a trust inside that if I let go of control, I will not descend into the unfathomable depths of depravity and indulgence and lose all focus and direction in my life. Slowly I notice that there is an inner force or guide that keeps the ship on course. I don't totally trust it yet but it is slowly coming.

You cannot run away from yourself.
Rather than run away, run withinwards,
Come closer to yourself to have a better look.
It is time to wake up.
You have wasted too much valuable time, energy, and opportunity already.
But there is still time and the moment you wake up
For you the night ends and the dawn begins.
Osho

Exercises:
1. Identifying addictiveness:
What behaviors do you do which are obsessive, perhaps self-destructive, and take you away from the present?

Pick one of these behaviors and notice:

- a.) Are you judging this behavior? If so, what is the judgment?
- b.) What stresses in your life trigger this behavior?
- c.) How is this addiction expressing a hidden fear or shame? See if you can connect with the fear or shame and feel it in the body.

2. Healing addictiveness:
Ask yourself,

- a.) "What is the price that I am paying for his behavior – in terms of my creativity, relationships, and physical health?"
- b. "Am I ready and willing to go through the fear, anxiety, shame and pain that will come up if I decide to heal?"

c. "How would my life, self-esteem, and relating benefit from taking this step?"
   d. "What concrete steps can I take in my life right now to get support to heal my addictiveness?"

Chapter 8:

MAGICAL THINKING

Years ago, when I started my own therapy, my therapist asked me to talk a bit about my childhood. I thought for a few moments and then said that there wasn't really much to say, "I had a great childhood." My therapist had her work cut out for her. I had idealized my parents to such an extent that I was still looking at the world through their eyes.

When in the course of my therapy, they began to fall from grace; it was a shocking experience for me. It was one of my first encounters with my aloneness. In our childhood state of mind, we idealize our caretakers because it gives us a foundation to face life and a strong sense of belonging. It is as though we live in a mystified state, in a kind of fantasy state, where we imagine things to be as we would like them to be.

Mystification is Natural for a Child
It is a necessary survival mechanism for a child because he or she has no other choice but to trust the "big people". But we don't grow out of it.

> *We remain mystified even as an adult, unable to see or evaluate reality clearly because we are still thinking through the eyes of this child.*

Some years ago, I was invited to attend a marriage. I knew them both, particularly the woman, because they had attended workshops with us. While I was happy for them that they were celebrating their togetherness, I had an intuition that their deciding to get married was premature. They were having problems and their decision was partly based on the hope that by getting married and making inspiring vows to each other that their difficulties would vanish. They didn't and two years later they separated. Their choosing to get married was coming from their mystified child.

We don't want to see objectively - it is too frightening and too painful. Instead we remain hoping and then get disappointed over and over again. Mystification is one of the hallmarks of the child state of mind. For years after my idealization broke, I went to the other direction. I wanted as little connection as possible with my family. Whenever I saw another man with the same Jewish conditioning that I had, it made me shrink away in embarrassment.

I have a close friend whose natural innocence endears him to people immediately. But he is also extremely gullible and constantly feels betrayed by people to whom he gave his trust. When we fall in love, most of the time, we are in magical thinking. We don't see the other person as he or she is. What we see in these situations is what we want to see because our child is so hungry to have his or her needs met.

Our hunger blinds us. Most of the time when relationships run into trouble it is because one or both people become disappointed and frustrated. They started the relationship in their bubble, magically believing that the other person was the man or woman of their dreams, only to be bitterly disappointed when the other one does not live up to their hopes and expectations. We have a similar dynamic with authority figures. First they are wonderful and perfect but when they do something that shatters our "trust", we degrade them. We never saw them as they were to begin with.

Whether we are putting people on a pedestal or knocking them off, it all comes from our magical thinking. Things are neither as bad or as good as we see them through this perspective. But in magical thinking, we always swing from one extreme to another over and over again until we sink into resignation. We never just see what is. When we are a child, we naturally need and want to believe that what the big people are showing and telling us is true.

The Mystified Child Becomes the Mystified Adult
Our natural innocence and trust and our longing to learn makes us open, receptive, and gullible subjects. In this space, we look up to those who teach us without any discrimination. We are mystified by their authority and by the image they hold for us in our eyes. All this is normal and natural. It only becomes a problem when we carry our childhood mystification into adulthood.

> *One important contributor to our carrying this magical thinking into our adulthood is that we did not learn effective mastery of our world and build strong confidence in our own unique abilities to discern what is true or untrue for us. Another is that we are unwilling to accept that we have to stand on our own feet and face the world alone.*

In the frame of mind of our emotional child, we seek for a parent to look up to and take care of us. We hunger for attention and to feel special in their eyes. Furthermore, we gain self-esteem by proxy - just by looking up to someone, by the feeling that we know them and imagining that they are what we strive for. (For years, I gained by self-esteem just from having my older brother as "my brother". Then, I continued this tendency by often finding myself bragging that "so and so was my friend" and that person was someone whom I respected and wanted to be like.) We don t have authentic self-esteem. Our inner sense of well-being is not coming from our own sense of self but from idealizing another person.

When he or she falls from grace, we suffer. We feel disappointed, abandoned, and betrayed but we also land into our own lack of self-esteem that was artificially propped up by the other person. Usually we don't have a clue that this is why we feel so miserable. We assume that we feel bad because the other person let us down. When we are mystified and idealizing someone, we are unable to see clearly both the positive and negative aspects in a balanced, mature way.

This can happen with everyone we relate to - with lovers, friends, bosses, teachers or hero figures. From this space, it is painful when we start to see their humanness - it makes us feel abandoned and forces us to grow up. Our emotional child inside does not want to do that. So often what happens is that we feel cheated when the person does not live up to our expectations and then we look for another person to idealize and fill the empty hole inside.

I have experienced this kind of magical thinking not only with my parents but also with friends and teachers that I have had. I was still magically hoping that people are always sensitive, understanding, kind, and considerate. When I saw that they are less "enlightened" than I thought, I was disappointed. Also, when I encountered a new teacher, someone whom I could learn new things from, I idealized them. I felt that this was the greatest, newest thing and the person was so wonderful, wise and deep - until I started to see through him or her and up came my disappointment. Today, when I go to learn from someone, I am much more sanguine. I learn what I can, recognizing that this person has something to teach me but I no longer need to idealize them or become mystified. I am able to see clearly the person's strengths and deficiencies, and learn from them all the same.

Perhaps the subtlest way our mystified self shows itself is in our spirituality. This is the area where our deepest longing can meet our deepest blindness. That's why there is so much fanaticism, passion, and even violence connected with it. A few years ago, I went to India to attend a three-week, "enlightenment course". I have been on the "awakening path" for a long time and I have earned some stripes! But close friends of mine told me that I absolutely had to go to this course. It promoted itself as such a powerful experience that "enlightenment" was guaranteed by the end. I am embarrassed to admit that I got hooked - I went and it cost me big bucks! I cannot speak for anyone else, but there is no question that it was my mystified self that went to that course. Amana thought I was a bit nuts but she also knows my passion to leave no stone unturned in my pursuit of truth. I could have left that little stone of "truth" unturned.

Be yourself, just yourself, simply yourself.
And remember, you are taking a big risk
When you declare that you are simply yourself.

You don't belong to any herd, any crowd.
The more dangerously you live, the more you live.
It is possible to live, in a single moment, the whole eternity,
If you are ready to live with totality risking all and everything.
Osho

Exercises: Working With Mystification
1. Pick someone in your life that is or was an authority figure for you. In what ways has this person disappointed you? Notice if you have idealized this person and if your disappointment arose from his or her not meeting your hopes and expectations.
2. In your past relationships, what caused you to lose trust in that person? In what ways were you not seeing the person for who he or she was?
3. In your spiritual path, in what ways have you discovered that you did not trust yourself?

Part 3:

THE INNER EXPERIENCE OF THE EMOTIONAL CHILD

Chapter 9:

EMPTINESS AND NEEDINESS

Before I could gain any distance from my own emotional child, I had to understand and experience his inner world. I started in total denial of his existence. I recall one poignant experience some years ago. I was doing a group for men. One of the processes we did was to dress as a woman and spend three days getting to know and feel what it felt like. At first, I stayed on the surface, spending time dressing in different outfits and prancing around with the novelty of it. But by the second day, something shifted and I began to feel more and more insecure, hidden and shy.

I could see that another part of me was coming out which I was not at all familiar with. From my normal gregarious, busy, speedy, and outward self, I slipped into a space where I became more silent, mistrustful, frightened, and ashamed. By the third day, I was becoming more comfortable and relaxed in this space and I was reluctant to switch back. What I see now is that in this process, I entered into the inner feelings of my emotional child. It was strange and uncomfortable but with time, I began to feel a softness and vulnerability with it.

Fear Is the Root of Our Emotional Behavior
When our emotional child takes over our consciousness, it does so with such a powerful and compelling energy that it is difficult to gain distance from it. But if we can step inside and

feel how strong these feelings are, it helps us to understand why it is such an overwhelming force in our life. And this understanding also helps us gain to space from it and not to judge ourselves when we are reactive, addictive, or full of expectations and fantasies. In the next chapters, we take you on a guided tour of what we have discovered is the inner landscape of the emotional child. You could imagine that it is like taking a journey down the river of the inner world of our child-self.

We begin by addressing the experience of negative emptiness of the emotional child and the neediness that naturally springs from it. Imagine yourself as a child. What do you feel would be some basic needs that you would like to have met from your parents?

Would they be? -
1. The need to feel wanted and to feel special and respected as a unique person (for who you are, not for what you do).
2. The need to have your feelings (e.g. fear, sorrow, anger, or pain), thoughts, and intuition validated.
3. The need to be seen, appreciated, encouraged, and inspired to discover your uniqueness as a person.
4. The need to be supported to develop your natural life energies of sexuality, creativity, joy, resourcefulness, power, playfulness, and celebration
5. The need to feel secure and safe.
6. The need to be physically touched with loving presence.
7. The need to be inspired and motivated to learn.
8. The need to know that it is okay to make mistakes and to learn from them.

9. The need to witness love and intimacy.
10. The need to be encouraged and supported to separate and find ourselves.
11. The need to be given firm and loving limits.

We call there "the essential needs".

As a child, we each have essential needs.
When these essential needs are not met,
we live in a constant state of deprivation.
That deprivation is the energetic hole
inside, longing to be filled.

We joke in our workshops that if you want to get in touch with how needy our wounded child is just imagine a hippopotamus with his mouth open saying, "Feed me!" Naturally, each one of us has our own story of deprivation depending on which essential needs we did not get. While the degree and types of deprivation vary, we all share a common experience of deprivation in some form.

And it is important to understand that no matter how perfect our parenting might have been, we would still experience neglect and deprivation. Without that feeling and healing from it, we would never grow up. Prior to that, from our deprivation, we unconsciously project our unmet needs on our lovers, close friends, on those we work with, on our children - in fact on anyone with whom we relate. The closer the connection, the deeper the projection.

This list is where our deprivation comes from. Each one of us is most sensitive about those needs on this list that were not met. We call these, *"our sensitivities."* When we go to another person, very often we are coming unconsciously with our sensitivities and we will even attract someone who will provoke us. When there is no awareness, we move automatically into one of the five behavior patterns of the emotional child. But as awareness develops, these behaviors become not so automatic.

When I have felt disturbed, (in other words when one of my essential needs is not being met), my natural and spontaneous response was to look for someone to blame. After twenty years of self-work, I began to recognize that blaming is a dark road. It leads to nowhere but conflict and pain. The compulsion to blame remains. But I can see that this is just my emotional child in "cruise control". And knowing that, allows me to make a choice. When I feel disturbed, there is more space now to watch and actually say to myself, "you know what, kid, you don't have to go into blame right now." Only rarely now is the process unconscious and out of control.

We spend much of our time and energy in our daily life unconsciously trying to fill the holes caused by our unmet needs as a child. Much of our behavior is directed at getting others to fill them. For example, Benjamin, a participant in a recent workshop we did in Denmark, had a compulsive need to socialize with people during the breaks, even calling friends at home on his cell phone. Even when we would make the suggestion that people should spend some time in silence integrating what was coming up, he found it very difficult to stay with himself. As we went more deeply into the process, he began to recognize that this compulsion was connected to his not having had anyone in his childhood to talk to.

Mary, in another workshop, would be the first person to raise her hand every time we had a group sharing. She was not aware that she had an insatiable need for attention and recognition, but as we uncovered her story, she could see that she never received the attention she needed as a child and now this longing runs her life.

One of my biggest sensitivities has always been one of not feeling validated for what I do and that is related to feeling compared unfavorably to by older brother. I spent a tremendous amount of energy and about five hundred years of schooling trying to prove to others and to myself that I was capable.

Those of us who did not receive the support we needed to find out who we were have a support sensitivity. When we did not get the recognition we needed, we have a recognition sensitivity. We have a worthiness sensitivity when we feel that we are not good enough as a person. Then we hunger for someone to validate us so that the hole can be filled.

We may have sensitivities connected to getting warmth and touch, and then we become dependent on someone to provide that for us. Or we may have a sensitivity related to trust. We may feel that to open and be vulnerable exposes us to mistreatment, control or manipulation from another. This sensitivity creates a co-dependency in which we are continually pushing other people away while longing for closeness at the same time.

Our unmet needs cause us to become highly sensitive to receiving this need today in our life. The unmet need created an emptiness inside that we compulsively attempt to fill from others. This emptiness creates deep anxiety and our life becomes a constant unconscious compulsion to fill it. It creates a dependency on the outside in some way either by desiring another or a situation to fill it or by avoiding a person or situation because of the hole.

Furthermore, the emptiness has a powerful effect on the type of people and situations we attract. We have a compulsion to create situations that provokes our emptiness because that is often the only way that we can become aware that it there. This is the way that we can learn and develop what is missing inside. We need the challenge to grow.

Here are some common sensitivities:
1. Feeling unwanted and abandoned
2. Not feeling special or respected
3. Not trusting your feelings
4. Lacking self motivation
5. Having deep fears of survival
6. Having a deep need for touch and closeness
7. Lacking motivation to learn
8. Craving love and attention
9. Being perfectionist and self-critical
10. Feeling engulfed and controlled

When we don't have awareness or understanding of our sensitivities and how they are affecting our life, we naturally feel that something on the outside has to change for us to be happy. This is one of the cardinal beliefs of the emotional self.

Emptiness is real. It exists. It comes from the past. *But how we relate to it makes all the difference in our lives.* If we believe that another person, a substance, or life has to fill it, we are lost. We may believe that people have to start treating us better, or give us more recognition, more love, more attention, more space and so on. We may go to a substance or an activity to soothe the emptiness. In the child state, we cannot imagine any other way to end the discomfort, pain, anxiety, and fear that the emptiness causes without filling it from the outside.

However, our efforts to fill our emptiness from the outside never work. This efforting only creates deeper frustration. It does help, however, to begin to understand that we have emptiness created from unmet needs in our past and to know what kind of behavior from people or life triggers us to most.

We Heal From Our Emptiness When We Feel It
Healing our holes begins when we recognize how robotically we try to fill them from the outside. This process of watching and understanding frees up energy to break the automatic behavior and just be with the experience of emptiness when it is provoked. Being with them means feeling them and letting them be there without trying to fix or change anything – in other words, just feeling the physical sensation of emptiness and observing the obsessive mind that goes with it.

In a recent workshop, a couple got into a conflict just before a break time. The man went into panic and asked for one of us to come and work with them just as people were going out to lunch. I told him that we would deal with it immediately in the group as a whole when we reconvened. During the lunch break, he has very disturbed and angry with me that I wasn't attending to him right away. After the group came together again, he expressed his anger and feelings of betrayal.

The situation had triggered many buried feelings. Whenever he quarrels with his wife, it brings up a deep panic that he will lose her. In his child state of mind, he has no space to contain the anxiety or the anger. After we dealt with the situation and brought some awareness to it, he was able to see his reaction with a bit of distance. Waiting for the lunch break to end perhaps helped him feel his needs and anxiety instead of acting out from his panic so automatically as he has always done.

> *"The reason one seeks attention*
> *Is because one does not know oneself.*
> *It is only in the other person's eyes*
> *One can see his face,*
> *In their opinions he can find his*
> *personality."*
> Osho

Exercise: Exploring Needs and Emptiness
1. Look over the essential need list. Ask yourself, "Do I have a sensitivity related to this need?"
2. Then focusing on this particular sensitivity, ask yourself, "How does it affect how I relate with people and life?"
3. Staying with this sensitivity, ask yourself, "How do I feel it inside when it gets provoked?"
4. Exploring Your Needs
   a.) What thoughts and feelings arise for you when consider your needs?
   E.g. "I don't feel I have the right to want or need this." "I am weak or needy if I want this." "If I show these needs, I will be taken advantage of." "Why bother to feel or express these needs, I'll never get them anyway."
   b.) Write down what beliefs you hold inside about having or expressing these needs.
   c.) What were you taught (verbally or non-verbally) as a child about having and expressing your needs. E.g. "Men should not have

or express their needs." "It is selfish to have needs and wants." "There are more important things in life to be concerned about than what you need."

Chapter 10:

FEAR

Kristin, a Norwegian friend of mine, is terrified of water. She has no idea where it comes from but just the idea of going into the ocean fills her with dread. It is very un-Norwegian. Nathan, another friend, is a gifted musician but whenever he performs, he is overcome with crippling stage fright. Andreas, a Swiss engineer who has come to many of our workshops, has a highly responsible job working for the city government in his town. But he is terrified to disagree or confront anyone in even the slightest way.

Most of us have unexplained and irrational fears. I have a recurrent dream that I am about to take an exam but I am unprepared, and another in which I am all alone and looking desperately for Amana but am unable to find her. When I explore spaces inside I find deep fear. I can attribute it to different reasons but basically it is just a feeling inside that can be easily triggered by small, seemingly insignificant, things. And it seems that the older and perhaps more sensitive I become, the frightened part of me feels even more intense. Sometimes I wake up at night with what feels like an attack of fear. I seldom know what it is or why is has come. I suspect that it was always there but I covered it so effectively that I could not feel or recognize it so clearly before. When it comes, I watch my breath and tell myself, "It's okay, don't fight it, it will pass." It does pass.

Fear is Deep, Irrational and Mysterious
Fear is another of the cardinal qualities of our emotional child. It is easier to appreciate why this inner part of us is so powerful once we understand how much fear we carry all the time. At a higher plane of awareness, we might begin to see that much of our fear is illusory and that much of it comes from our past experiences. We might even know that we are all in the lap of a benevolent existence. I know all about the fact that fear is often a product of past conditioning and past traumas. I also know most of the time that there is nothing rational driving my fear. I have even had many glimpses that there is nothing to fear and deep inside know this to be true. Still, for the most part, it is not part of my everyday reality.

Once I stopped running away from my fears so compulsively, I have been amazed at how strong it feels at times. And I have noticed that there is an undercurrent of chronic fear inside of me most of the time. This fear can be augmented by stress, setbacks, criticism, or loss but only because it is there already. I suspect that many, if not most of us, have profound fear inside that we may cover with all kinds of compensations and distractions.

Sometimes, we may feel fear as restlessness, anxiety, or panic. But many times, we don't experience the fear directly, we feel it as some kind of disturbance or contraction in the body, such as shortness of breath, irritability, short temper, problems with digestion, burning in the stomach and so on. Fear in its frozen form (shock) can also cause paralysis, sexual dysfunction, inability to speak or stuttering, confusion, and forgetfulness.

Fear From Past Traumas Lives in the Nervous System

Fear, other than that which comes to us when confronted with immediate danger, is based on the past. It comes from experiences and conditioning which lives in our mind and in the nervous system. Our mind has become imprinted by negative experiences, traumas, and by the fearful thought forms of our parents, teachers, and culture. Now, the fears that are dormant in our nervous system can be triggered by some event or stimulus that reminds us of an earlier trauma. And this process is usually totally unconscious.

By observing my fears closely, without judgment, I come to recognize that, most of the time; they have little or no basis in reality. Sometimes, I can identify that a fear came from one or both of my parents and how it has subtly crept into my own thinking. For example, when I was young, the fears of money and survival were always prevalent even though we never had to struggle financially. But most of the time, there is little awareness between the stimulus and the original trauma.

Accepting Fear Starts with Acknowledging It

To accept fear, our first step is to acknowledge that it is there. There is a story that my father used to tell when I was a child. It is a story of a little boy who was terrified of "kreplach". "Kreplach" are Jewish ravioli. One day, his mother took him aside and said to him that she was going to show him that there was nothing to be afraid of with "kreplach". She took him into the kitchen and sat him down. Rolling out a piece of dough, she asked him if he was afraid.

"No," he replied. She cut out a little square of the dough.

"Anything to be afraid of?" she asked.
"Nope." Then she took a bit of ground meat and placed in the middle of the dough.
"Anything?"
"No, of course not!" he answered.
Then she took one corner and folded it over.
"Are you scared?" she asked.
"No." She took another corner and folded it over.
"Scared yet?"
"Nope." She took the third corner and folded it over.
"Scared?"
"No." Finally, she took the last corner and folded in over.
"Ahhhh, Kreplach!!!!"

That's how fear can often be, as irrational as looking at "kreplach" and arriving as suddenly and as unpredictably as well.

There Are Reasons For Our Fear

The second aspect of learning to accept fear is realizing that there are ample reasons for having it even if we don't know what the reasons are. There are multiple sources of our child's fear. First of all, for a sensitive being, it is not possible to grow up in our stressful, repressed, competitive, moralistic, Western world without developing deep fears. Then there is the trauma of birth into a physical body and the way in which most of us were born. The countless traumas we experienced in childhood only added to this original birth trauma. Any harshness or invasion even of the subtlest kind is totally shocking to us in our natural sensitivity. Finally, there is simply the insecurity of living in a world where we are basically helpless in relation to the greater forces of life.

> *There is no way to avoid the traumas of childhood no matter how perfect are parenting is. We heal, not by blaming or resenting people or situations that traumatized us, but by realizing and feeling their impact.*

If we put ourselves in the shoes of a small child and imagine what it must have been like in this state to go through these experiences, we begin to feel the impact of trauma. By going through that process, I have developed compassion for myself. It has made me more human and I don't regret or resent anything that happened to me. In fact, recovering from painful past experiences makes us stronger, more human, more compassionate, and more alive.

The Two Basic Fears

We have many fears but underlying all of them are two basic fears. One is of *not surviving*. And the second is of *not receiving love*. All other fears are just out-croppings of these two. When we start to examine our fears and our behavior more closely, we come to see that much of our life is oriented around these two fears one way or another. Our culture does not teach a graceful approach to fear. What we learn is to deny it and to push through it. We may struggle to present an image that convinces others and ourselves that our fears don't exist and feel shame for having them. We may pressure ourselves or judge ourselves for our fears.

But if we don't have a friendly acceptance of our fears, we don't have a friendly relationship to our sensitivity either. And if we don't have a flowing way to deal with our fears, we never learn a healthy relationship to our power.

We may consider power as the absence of fear rather than a natural acceptance of it.

With this negative conditioning about fear, we learn to feel shame for our sensitivity and vulnerability instead of appreciating the beauty of these qualities. Our power becomes aggressive rather than centered.

Recognizing Our Inner Split
I had compensated for my fears so effectively that once in college when a roommate dropped out of school and started to see a psychiatrist, I just thought he was weak. It was not until many years later that I began to recognize the split that I had created inside. On the surface, I had crafted very creative masks to perform and keep everything together but underneath, I was hiding a deeply frightened child. This frightened child would come up in stressful situations such as in relating to women, taking exams or competing in sports.

When I took the SATs (the exams that you have to take for entering into a university in the US), I got so nervous that I could not read the questions on the page. Once in college, (I managed to get in anyway), I asked a very sexy and attractive girl in one of my classes for a date. I was very surprised that she said yes but when I picked her up, I was so nervous that I had trouble thinking of anything to talk about. Everything seemed just not "cool" enough. As the evening went on, I got more and more tense until finally when we went to a party given by some friends, I started drinking much more than I could handle. Which isn't much. Finally, feeling a bit sick, I excused myself to step outside but she insisted on accompanying me. Once outside, I mustered the courage to kiss her but then vomited (almost all over her). That was the end of what might have been a budding relationship.

I guess many of us have horror stories like that. When we have repressed our sensitive side, it can come out in unexpected and surprising ways or we can project it on to a lover. I did that too. My first love was a deeply sensitive person who had spent years in therapy just to find the strength and confidence to live from one day to the next. Dealing with life was a constant challenge for her. I could not understand why she was having such difficulty since I believed that the best way to overcome fear was just to push through it. I thought that she was just indulging her fears.

> *When our tough compensating side condemns our sensitive side for its fears, our sensitive side hides or takes revenge with subtle sabotage. It becomes a constant inner fight.*

On a deeper level, we may be afraid that if we accept our fear, it will take over our life. I have a strong warrior inside who refuses to give into fear and continually creates challenges for me to overcome it. That's a good quality but only if our warrior has deep understanding and compassion for our frightened side. By exploring my fears, they didn't become more powerful as I expected. Quite the contrary.

Feeling Fear in the Body
The third part of learning to deal with fear is beginning to recognize how it feels in our mind and body when it appears. When we become irritable or speedy, it is always good sign that our frightened child has taken over. When our fear takes hold, we can experience it by becoming aggressive,

hyperactive, hyper-vigilant, speedy, anxious, or even in panic. We can shake; our heart beats faster, our chest contracts, our breath gets shallow, our palms sweat, we can become confused, frozen, numb, or paralyzed. And we can begin to obsess about everything and anything. If something such as a rejection, criticism, loss, disappointment, or failure triggers our fear, our mind can begin to ruminate compulsively with the most dreadful scenarios. Watching fear compassionately means observing these mind and body phenomena with a loving and understanding heart.

> *"You feel fear.*
> *Now the fear is an existential reality,*
> *An experiential reality;*
> *It is there.*
> *You can reject it;*
> *By rejecting it you will be repressing it.*
> *By repressing it, you will create a wound in*
> *your being."*
> Osho

Exercises:
Exploring Fear
1. Begin by writing down or bringing awareness to your deepest fears in relation to:
    a. Coming close to another person
    b. Expressing your creativity
    c. Being secure financially

Ask yourself; in what ways do these fears come from how I was taught to think? In what ways do these fears come from traumatic experiences in my past?

2. With your non-dominant hand (imagining that it is your inner child talking) write down what your fears are and why they are there.
3. How do you feel about having these fears? Do you judge them? If so, what are your judgments?
4. What was the message that you received (verbally or non-verbally) about how to deal with fears? Minimize them? Push yourself to overcome them? Don't give in to them? Give in to them?
5. Is there a split inside between a side of you that pushes and judges and another side that has fear? Describe this split in a picture. How do you deal with this split?

A Simple Meditation on Dealing with Fear
When you notice that fear is arising, take a moment to close your eyes. Allow yourself to settle by noticing and feeling the breath as it comes and goes. You can even count the breaths coming and going up to twenty.

Then turn your attention to how you experience the fear in the body. Notice the quality of your breath – it is shallow or full. Notice your chest – does it feel tight or relaxed. Notice your solar plexus and your belly – is it tight or relaxed.

Now notice what specific thoughts are connected to the fear. (We call them "the fear thoughts".) As you become aware of each thought, consciously let it go, watching it dissolve like a cloud disappearing.

Now come back to your breathing, your chest and your belly. Has anything changed?

Chapter 11:

THE INFECTION

Some years ago, I was doing an intense therapy workshop that was focused on childhood de-conditioning. One of the most significant discoveries I made in that experience was that many of my fears were really my mother's fears. I knew this intellectually but I had never truly experienced it so vividly. I have always been very closely bonded with her and as a result, I unknowingly saw the world through her eyes. In our work, we call this phenomenon of taking on the feelings and thought forms of those who raised us - *"the infection"*.

> *The infection is all the ways that our energy has been negatively affected by our conditioning. It is all the repressive beliefs and fears that we unknowingly brought inside, all the negative expectations and feelings of limitation that we breathed in from our significant caretakers.*

As a child, we are a helpless receptacle of all the fears and negativity of our caretakers and of the repressive society that each of us were raised in. We call it "an infection" because it entered our thoughts and body without our knowing it and spread to affect our energy, our self-esteem, creativity, relationships, sexuality, and intelligence - in short, all aspects of our lives.

The Infection Explains Our Negative Patterns
The infection helps to explain a great deal about the inner experience of the emotional child. It is often hard to understand otherwise how we have so much fear, shame, inhibition and self-doubt inside. The infection helps clarify how we find ourselves repeating lifestyles and patterns that belonged to one or both of our parents. Of course not everything we were infected with was negative. Many of our positive qualities were in part inherited in some mysterious way. But we focus here at how our emotional child developed its fears, shame and mistrust and a good part of it came from the infection. Another term that is used for the phenomenon that we call, "the infection" is "negative merging". In our innocence and helplessness as a child, we naturally merge with those who are taking care of us. When what we merge with is contaminated with fears and negativity, this merging is negative.

If we explore any specific fear or behavior pattern, we can often trace it back to a fearful attitude or behavior of one of our caretakers. The ways that our fears are expressed in our life today often mirror how one or both of our parents related to and expressed fears. Our negative and judgmental attitudes toward others and life in general often reflect similar attitudes of our parents. Our attitudes toward money, sexuality, success, or playfulness can be traced back to our conditioning, to the beliefs we learned from our parents, teachers, priests or other significant people who brought us up. Prior to exploring our inner world, we may never have even thought that these beliefs didn't fit us. And the source of our infection goes far deeper than simply what we absorbed from our early caretakers. It is in the very air we breathe. The repression, negative beliefs, defensiveness, competition, and pressure is deeply embedded in our culture. We can't avoid it.

The Infection Becomes Our Identity
Another way of understanding the infection is to see that we were each cast in a mold according to all these reflections, repressions, beliefs and behaviors that were transmitted to us. We literally became, as we were supposed to become. And that is now how we think about and feels ourselves. We behave as automatons acting out the script that we were given. The infection made the mold and all our concepts of who we are is the sculpture that came from this mold. It is unimaginable for us to think or behave any differently. That is just who and how we are.

Some years ago, Amana and I, while traveling from one workshop to another, spent the night with a friend who was caretaking a large villa outside of Florence. The people who lived there, an American family living in Europe, were away on a trip. The husband of this family was a busy executive who was seldom at home and the wife was living in this enormous house mostly alone with her two children. She complained frequently to our friend of how angry she was because of her situation. On the wall in their bedroom was a personalized certificate from the Pope blessing their marriage.

I realized that this whole situation - a marriage based on unconsciousness and a family living together without any real love or connection was such a predictable consequence of their infection. Both had come from strictly religious families where their parents had lived together without consciousness or connection. They seemed to be mimicking the life of their parents.

It takes tremendous courage to discover our infection, let alone break free of it. It is unquestionably the single most courageous step we will ever take in our life. Our conditioning - the religion, culture, class we were raised in - gives us an identity. And until we start to break away, we usually don't realize how it is crushing us or even that there is any other way to live that differs from what we were taught. The judgments and pressure that came with our infection were very deep and very insidious. We may have spent a lifetime believing that the voices of our inner and outer critics were true and believing that our inadequacies are who we are. Our infection happened so early and so deeply that we never knew ourselves any differently. We think that our infected self is who we are. It is our deepest identification.

Some of the people who attend our workshops in different countries around the world continue to go deeper with our work. Knowing and watching their progress over a period of several years gives us a chance to see profound changes in their lives. In some countries, Turkey, China, or Taiwan for example, even the act of coming to such a workshop is revolutionary for them.

But regardless of the country and conditioning they come from, during this time, many of them find themselves making big changes in their lives - often giving up jobs that no longer suit them, ending or altering relationships, especially with their family of origin, that were based on old ways of being and changing their priorities from doing to being.

Making these changes takes time and patience. From the space of our sensitive and vulnerable side, it is terrifying to break from what we were taught. To our emotional child, it can feel like the threat of abandonment, punishment and perhaps eternal damnation. To this part of us, adhering to these beliefs and behaviors is life itself - survival and belonging. To separate from them means isolation and starvation.

The Infection Can Be Hidden
There are patterns in our behavior that we adopted for reasons and in ways that are mysterious and perhaps can never be explained. Sometimes we cannot discover why we act the way we do. The reasons can be buried in family secrets or tendencies that we became infected with very mysteriously.

For example, a son or daughter of an alcoholic may have strong addictive tendencies in stressful situations. Another person whose parents were strictly religious and harshly judgmental and repressive may find him or herself having similar rigidities. A son or daughter of a hypochondriac may find himself also plagued with fears of illness. A child of a suicidal parent may have similar thoughts. And so on. Sometimes, these behaviors and tendencies can even be traced to grandparents or other relatives. Or a child can be acting out a family secret and only once the secret is revealed, is the person able to explain his behavior or beliefs.

Recovering From the Infection
The deeper we explore our infection, the more and more subtle we discover how much our attitudes, behavior and energy have been affected. We need to examine every single belief and attitude we hold to see whether it belongs to us or is part of our infection. This includes gradually exploring our attitudes about sex, feelings, power, wildness, responsibility,

spirituality, relationship, marriage, caring for the body, eating, learning, money, and work. When we start to look at all these things with this question in mind, slowly we disinfect ourselves. If it feels right in the belly, it is ours, if not, it is the infection. But it might not be possible at first to feel if something feels right in the belly. In my experience, it took time to develop this awareness.

It has been helpful to return periodically to my roots to see what was mine and what was not. Whenever I visited with members of my family, it was a renewed opportunity to observe my infection. First, I needed to get far away for a long time before I could feel strong enough even to go back at all. Breaking away from all my conditioning began almost thirty years ago when I dropped out of medical school. That was, in some ways, the most significant and courageous step I ever took because I was able to see, at that time, that I was not leading my own life.

It began a process of finding myself, which still continues today. My priorities changed from success to inner truth. Eventually, I went back to medical school and then on to do residencies in Family Medicine and Psychiatry but things were never the same. I had stepped off of the train and I would never get on again.

Working through our infection is a bit like slaying a dragon. Our conditioning is a big fire-breathing monster, which threatens to extinguish us with flames if we step out of line.

Our emotional child does not have the courage to fight this dragon. But another space inside of us does. Our "seeker" is the Jason, the Hercules of our being. We will be dealing with this aspect of our being in a later chapter. But no matter how strong our seeker is, if we want to stay connected with our sensitivity, we have to also stay connected to the fears of our emotional child.

In my experience, if our intention to find ourselves is sincere, the behavior and beliefs that are not ours will slowly fall away. The life force inside of us will naturally assert itself in spite of our fears. It is also a delicate matter when we become aware of how deeply conditioned we have been and how strongly we have been influenced by life negative attitudes and behaviors. It is easy to get lost in anger, resentment and blame.

We need to feel the way our conditioning has shut down our energy and our feelings but at the same time, it does not serve us to harbor blame and resentment. I found that I needed to go through a rage period where I allowed myself to feel my anger and resentment toward those who raised me. But then, there came a time when I was ready to let go of this anger and resentment and honor both my parents and my roots for the gifts, beauty, and love that I received.

> *"Every generation goes on giving its diseases*
> *To the new generation, and naturally,*
> *The new generation becomes more and more burdened.*
> *You are the inheritor of all the repressive concepts*
> *Of the whole of history."*
> Osho

Exercises: Exploring the Infection

1. Examining each belief and behavior about the following areas (and write them down) - sex,

spirituality, power, individuality, feelings, money, giving, relationship and marriage, responsibility and freedom, family, eating and the body, work, and relaxation.
2. Ask Yourself:
   a. Who does this come from?
   b. Did my parents have the same attitude?
   c. Review the beliefs in relation to the class, religion, and culture that you were raised in.
   d. What would it be like if I don't listen to this belief or don't behave as I think I should behave?

Chapter 12:

SHAME AND GUILT

Another of the cardinal inner experiences of our emotional child is shame and guilt. Shame is the inner feeling of not being enough. I suspect each of us has our own words to describe this inner experience. But however we may describe it, it doesn't feel good.

When I have been taken over by my shame, I could not even feel myself. I not only didn't have a positive experience of myself, I didn't have *any* experience of myself. My energy would sink, everything would seem like too much effort. I could not imagine that I could be competent at anything and or that anyone could love and respect me. If someone would ask me "what do you feel?" it would be as though he or she was speaking a language that I had no clue about.

To make matters worse, I would begin to behave in ways that fortified these feelings. I might say stupid things, make all kinds of mistakes, begin leaving messes around and not complete things I was doing or do them in a shoddy way, perhaps even walk around in a daze. Then I would feel guilty for being such a drag and go deeper into the hole. From this space, I would look out and see a world where everyone else was successful but I would always be a total failure. When I was in this space, I normally could not imagine that there was anything else. I believed that this was who I was, this is how life is and nothing will ever change.

One day, while in the middle of writing this chapter, I was sitting in a hair salon in Sedona, Arizona where we live, waiting to get a haircut. A woman was just finishing having her hair done. I watched as she got up from the chair, paid and left. She stopped very briefly to look at herself in the mirror and walked away so that no one would see her. She was actually an attractive woman but held her body and walked in such a way that I could tell that she didn't think so.

If we hold a mirror in front of ourselves, the first impression is usually that of shame. Invariable, we will find something that is not right and needs to be improved. Remember the last time that you felt excluded or that you didn't belong somewhere? Or the last time you were rejected or failed in something significant? Or you were with someone whom you looked up to and said something inappropriate? Or you were with someone you respected and you just could not feel yourself? These moments provoke our shame. Can you remember what these experiences felt like? When shame takes us over, we feel that we are not okay the way we are. We may feel our shame acutely in what we call, "shame attacks", but it is basically there all the time. For some of us, our shame actually cripples us.

The Shame Voices

Our shame is fortified by voices inside which are constantly evaluating us and reminding us that we are defective and that we have to change to be better, to make it, to be a winner, to succeed. We call this the "pusher-judge" which we will be addressing in greater detail in the next chapter. Without our shame, the pusher-judge could not exist. Our shame tells us that everything that the "pusher-judge" says is the absolute truth.

The most crippling aspect of shame is that it cuts us off from feeling ourselves – it cuts us off from our center. Shame makes us feel disconnected from the experience of being at home inside. And for many of us, we have felt so shamed for so long that we have never known what it was to feel at home inside. We are identified with our shame.

Recently, I attended a three-year training in healing trauma consisting of three four-day trainings a year. Because of our intense schedule leading workshops, I had to attend each section in different places, with different teachers and always with new people. I noticed, especially in the beginning, that I felt extremely insecure. Unable to hide behind my accustomed role as a workshop leader, I could feel myself awkward and like a newcomer on the block. When people broke for lunch, I wanted to be included in one of the parties going out together but was too ashamed to ask if I could come along. Finally, I overcame my pride and risked to ask and people received me openly and lovingly. It helped to know that this was shame that I was feeling, that it was natural since I was new and also striped of my roles. I allowed myself to feel it and by asking people if I could join them, to admit it, somehow. By the third day, I felt included and my shame disappeared.

"Winner" or "Losers" Are Equally in Shame

We all have shame, but each of us has dealt with it differently. For some of us, our shame is on the surface and we are constantly plagued with feelings of inadequacy. We may be deeply identified with being a "loser". Others of us alternate between feeling worthless or adequate depending on how we are doing in the world. Successes take us up and failures take us down. We go back and forth between feeling inferior or superior, a "winner" or a "loser", depending on the feedback we get. That has always been the case with me.

There are still others of us who have compensated so well for our shame by being "successful" that we see others as the "losers" while we believe that we are the "winners". But for those who have effectively compensated for their shame, all it takes is a profound trauma such as a loss, rejection, illness, accident, or exhaustion for such a person to look deeper and discover the shame inside behind his or her masks.

I have always lived with the belief that when thoughts and feelings of worthlessness and failure arise, don't give into them, try harder! My shame was always there but I believed that to give in to it was a sign of weakness and laziness. Furthermore, if I let go into it, I will never get out. I could see no value to allowing myself to feel shame. But I have come to see that when we don't take a journey into our shame, we cannot find ourselves. Whether we collapse in shame or compensate to overcome it, our inner life remains driven by shame.

A friend, who happens to be a beautiful and attractive woman, told me of an incident where she was organizing a workshop for someone. Shortly after the workshop leader arrived, he asked if she would like to spend the night together. She acknowledged that there was "energy" between them but told him that she didn't feel to go to bed together. She was in a committed relationship and felt that when she checked inside, she did not want to sleep with other men. He continued to pester her to sleep with him and was unable to hear or accept her rejection. Accustomed to getting his way with women in such cases, he was not used to rejection and even less inclined to admit or feel his shame.

On the journey of true self-discovery, we have to become deeply intimate with this profound feeling inside which says, "I am inadequate, I am a failure and therefore I must hide my inadequacies or others will know the truth about me." It is a crucial part of the journey because it makes us human. It is a kind of rite of passage. When I cover my shame with compensations, I start to feel that I am running away from myself. There is an ever-present fear lurking under the surface, which does not go away in spite of all our efforts to overcome it. This becomes an endless struggle because until we deal with the underlying fear and insecurity of shame, we are never at home with ourselves.

The Shame Cycle
Much automatic behavior comes from our shame. With a shamed identity, we don't trust ourselves and we feel dependent on others for esteem, love and attention. We become pleasers, doers, rescuers - whatever role and behavior gives us what we so desperately need to cover the emptiness that the shame brings. I have believed that my value and nourishment depended on what I did - without my achievements, I would be a nobody. Woman may often identify their value with how giving or loving they are while men often evaluate themselves by what they perform.

Our shame wound puts us in a shame bubble. From this bubble, we see the world as a dangerous, competitive jungle where there is only struggle and no love. From this bubble, we also believe that unless we struggle, compete, and compare, we will not survive. And finally, from our shame bubble, we believe that others are better, more loveable, more successful, more competent, more intelligent, more attractive, more powerful, more sensitive, more spiritual, more heartfelt, more courageous, more aware, and so on. All these thoughts about the world and other people also perpetuates our shame because it effects how people see us and relate to us. The message we broadcast from our shame bubble is basically, "I am not lovable or respectable so you can reject, abuse, or take advantage of me anyway and anytime you like."

From our shamed sense of self, we go to others looking for validation. We live in compromise. We relate from compromise. As we become used to seeing ourselves as someone who compromises, our shamed self-image deepens. This behavior invites rejection and makes us feel even less self-esteem. From. a fractured self-image, our inner tension builds and we can easily move into some form of addictive or compulsive behavior. All of this just adds to our shame.

The Shame Cycle

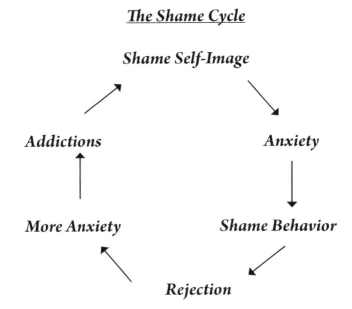

While shame is a phenomenon that affects us globally, it is also something, which we can observe more strongly in some areas of our life and less in others. Some of us, because of our past, may have deep shame and insecurity connected to our body, sexuality, creativity, courage, self-expression, being a parent, or toward our feelings and sensibilities. This shame affects how we relate and often keeps us from opening ourselves at all. We may feel it as a deep scar in our being and feel hopeless to overcome it. From our shame, we have perpetual guilt. We are always feeling that we have done something wrong.

On one level, much of what we believe about ourselves from our shame appears to be true. The shame voices seem to be validated by life experiences. We feel unlovable and we get rejected. We feel like a coward and we can see ourselves shrinking from taking risks. We feel fat and we are overweight. We feel that we have nothing valuable to give and we experience being judged or criticized. If it is so self-fulfilling how do we get out? How can we penetrate the lie of shame?

Is There Positive Shame?
We are often asked in our work if there is any such thing as positive shame. In other words, can the feelings, thoughts, and body experience that shame brings not also be sometimes a productive message. The answer is a qualified "yes". If we have behaved in a way that was insensitive, if we have done something without proper preparation and totality, shame can be a signal. It can be a signal that we have not lived up to our own standards of being kind and sensitive or doing something with the kind of energy that we feel is required. But even so, the message we internalize in these cases needs

to be gentle, loving, forgiving or ourselves, and motivate us to learn from this experience.

Getting Out of the Shame Bubble
This has been a profound question for me and also crucial to our work. What I have learned is that I slowly penetrate the lie by understanding. I know that shame is a product of my mind that has been conditioned in a repressive, moralistic, competitive, materialistic, and life negative culture. It is the product of a child who was raised in an environment where my being was not recognized and supported. As a result of this conditioning, I disconnected from my essential qualities and energies and lost touch with my center. Through understanding and feeling the shame when it arises, we get space from it.

Here are some simple steps for healing shame:

a) Feeling the Shame
Shame is not a comfortable feeling. It can make us feel heavy, dull, sleepy, and depressed. It covers our life energy like a heavy blanket and we lose contact with ourselves. In shame, we don't trust or even know what we feel, think, say, need or intuit. Our mind fills up with what we call, "shame voices" - the voices of the pusher-judge. These voices condemn and criticize us. We are overcome with mistrust - both for ourselves and others.

The "shame voices" not only condemn us but everyone and everything outside of us as well. The world appears as a hostile and dark place. With this kind of menu, why would anyone want to stick around to feel it? Far better, we think, to avoid it anyway we can. By taking the space inside to feel it and watch it when it comes, it heals. It brings a depth and sensitivity. We are feeling and watching the shamed child inside of us and inside of everyone. We set in motion an alchemical process of healing simply by being with the shame experience when it comes without changing anything.

b) Identifying the Triggers

Once we begin to recognize that we have shame and give ourselves the space to feel it when it arises, we can also start to identify the triggers. The triggers are what provoke our shame. Sometimes they are obvious and sometimes very subtle. It may be rejection; it may be how someone talks to us or looks at us. It may be situations where we feel inferior or humiliated. Or we may get triggered when we don't fulfill someone's expectations. There are many shame triggers. Our personal triggers have much to do with our original story of shaming.

c) Knowing Our Shame Story

When we begin to understand how we got shamed, we bring tremendous compassion to ourselves. We begin to understand that there is nothing wrong with us; our feelings of inadequacy come from our shaming. Shaming occurs when a child's natural spontaneity, self-love, and aliveness are shut down and when his or her essential needs are not met. It occurs as result of abuse, condemnation, comparison, or expectation placed on us as a child. It also occurs when the child is infected with the repression, fears and life negative attitudes of his or her parents or the culture in which he is raised. And it occurs with abandonment and any kind of abuse. Each of us had our own unique experience of shaming and rarely anyone escapes. Often, our caretakers raised us in the most loving and well-intended way. But they also were shamed and unknowingly pass the shame on to us.

d) Recognizing Our Compensations.

We get deep insight into our shame when we begin to recognize the ways that we run away from it. Each of us has our own way of not feeling the shame and covering it up but basically, at any time, we fall into one of two categories. We either puff up or we deflate. When we are puffing up, we are pushing ourselves to do better, be better, work harder, make a better impression, get the job, climb the ladder, keep on the move etc.

When we puff up, we push our energy to make sure that the shame will not take over. Somewhere, even the most hard-core puffers fear the ever-present threat of their shame taking over and as a result they can never relax. Deflating is the flip side of puffing up. We give up and collapse. Rather than keeping up the struggle of puffing, deflating is throwing in the towel. Some of us gave up a long time ago because it was too shocking and too painful to keep up the struggle. Or we give up in some areas and puff up in others.

e) Coming Out of the Bubble

The next aspect of recovering from shame is realizing that it is not who we are. Yes, it has an emotional reality, it can take over our mind, our sense of self, and our energy, but it is not intrinsic to our nature. However, if we take this step before we have deeply felt and embraced our shame, it can easily become a concept and a form of denial. Our shamed inner child will always feel that there is something wrong with him or her. But bringing awareness to the different aspects of our shame - how it feels, how it gets provoked, where it came from and how we run away from it - we start to dis-identify from it.

We can even say to ourselves,

> *"This is my shame. It is not who I am but right now, I feels strong and convincing. I chose to step back from it, watch and feel it. I give it up to the universe and go on with my living my life's vision."*

We begin to see that the shamed child may always feel deeply inadequate, can never do enough to get people to appreciate and love him or her and who has spent a lifetime covering up for his or her insecurities.

We call this, "stepping out of the bubble." There was a time when I couldn't imagine myself as someone with dignity or someone who had centeredness inside. But it came. Of course there are moments when I am overtaken with shame and I lose connection with this feeling, but it returns quickly. This feeling does not have to do with what I do. It is something else. How one can we reconnect with the "Yes" inside. The "Yes" is our nature. By learning to watch our negative mind without judging or trying to change it, this natural "Yes!" experience arises on its own.

f) Taking Small Risks

The last ingredient of coming out of the shame bubble involves taking small risks that challenge our old way of living and seeing ourselves. The shame confines us to living, thinking, and behaving in a familiar way, one that perpetuates shame on the shame cycle. When we take a risk, we break the cycle of negativity. This risk can be just about anything – communicating when we would normally isolate, making love in a way that challenges our conditioning, taking a trip away from home and country, having new kind of friends, starting a new activity and so on.

I have a dear friend who is now a therapist with a thriving practice in Oslo. But prior to this, he worked for eleven years as a manager in a chocolate factory. He was so miserable when he was in this job that he used to shut himself up in his office and eat chocolate until he felt ill. We now joke in our work that going through our shame is like surviving "eleven years in the chocolate factory".

> *"The child - every child around the earth,*
> *in all the societies –*
> *Is forced to renounce his being,*
> *Is forced to accept other's opinions about himself.*
> *Every child is born absolutely accepting himself as he is.*
> *Each child is born with great love for himself;*
> *He has self-love, self-respect because he is not yet a mind."*
> Osho

Exercises:
1. Locating Our Areas of Shame

Shame can hit us at all levels of our being. In this exercise, you can bring awareness to specific areas of your shame. With each area, note or write down any feelings of shame, inferiority, insecurity, or inadequacies you feel.

    a. Sexuality - e.g. Potency, orgasm, interest, fears.
    b. Body and Appearance - e.g. Shape and size, attractiveness, age, dress.

c. Survival - e.g. Ability to earn money, security.
d. Feelings - e.g. Ability to feel sadness, openness, sensitivity.
e. Power - e.g. assertiveness, ability to feel and express anger, knowing and expressing what you want, or being irresponsible, lazy, collapsed, or controlled by fears.
f. Joyfulness - e.g. Ability to be spontaneous, feeling too serious or responsible.
g. Creativity - e.g. Recognizing and able to express your gifts.
h. Clarity - e.g. living your life as you want, knowing your priorities in life.

2. Awareness of Compensations

How have you dealt and how do you deal with your shame? How do you deal with your fears?
   a. With yourself - Do you pretend that it is not there? Judge yourself? Collapse? Push faster and harder?
   b. With Others - Pull away into your own world? Fight or attack? Try to please? Be a compulsive entertainer? Defend yourself?
   c. Find some way to distract yourself – with some substance or some activity?

3. Coming Out of the Bubble.

Can you identify what it is like for you when you are gripped by shame?
   a. What does it feel like?
   b. What does the world seem like to you when in a shame trance?

  c. What do you think that others think of you?
  d. What do you think about yourself?
  e. What do you want from others?
(The more you can identify the shame state, the easier it becomes to dis-identify from it.)

Chapter 13:

THE PUSHER-JUDGE

My therapist friend in Oslo tells a story of an uncle of his who was the captain of a boat sailing in the East. An Indian who worked for him on the boat would inform him whenever he did something, "Sir, I have done this job up to your very high standards." We never do anything that can satisfy our "very high standards", but we never stop trying.

One of the strongest factors that keeps us bonded to believing that we are a frightened and shamed-based person is our inner "Pusher-Judge". It is the flip side of our shame. The "Pusher-Judge" is there to ensure that we follow the rules, standards and guidelines of our conditioning. When we don't it, it fills us with guilt, shame, and fear. The pushing energy comes in the form of inner voices, which may be verbal or just energetic, telling us continually to do more, be more, try harder and so on.

The judging energy comes in the form of voices telling that we are not enough in all sorts of ways - not smart enough, pretty enough, spiritual enough, not sensitive enough; not surrendered enough, not courageous enough, etc. It is constantly telling us what to do, what not to do, constantly evaluating and judging us for what we do or don't do, driving us, condemning us or criticizing us. Sometimes we don't hear this energy as voices but we may recognize it when we collapse or feel listless and without motivation.

These attacks can come from the outside or from voices inside our head. Our child heard the voices of our parents, teacher, religion or culture saying, "you should do this, you shouldn't do that, you are too much, you are not enough." We took all this in and translated into, "I should do this, I shouldn't do that, I am too much, I am not enough." Often, the admonitions, judgments, and criticisms of the pusher-judge came so long ago or came in such a nonverbal way that we do not hear them as "you" but only as "I". And we may not even be aware that we are under the thumb of the "Pusher-Judge." It is just life. Or we think that it is "God" talking to us. Over all the years of our punitive and moralistic conditioning, "God" has gotten some bad press.

Each of us has this energy complex in different ways and each of us acts it out in some combination of inner voices and outer projections. As long as we believe what this pusher-judge says to us, we will always find people on the outside to enhance it and plague us. At those moments, we feel abused and unseen, not realizing that they are just outward vocalizations of what we carry inside. If we have a harsh inner critic, as many of us do, we often become moralistic, judgmental, righteous and critical of others as well. The harsher our "Pusher-Judge," the more opinionated and tenacious we become about our points of view.

Ways the "Pusher-Judge" Shows Itself
1. *Inner Voices and Feelings of Pressure, Judgment and Criticism*
2. *Strict and Harsh Standards, Ideals, Morals toward Self*
3. *Outer Voices (Projected on Authority, Friends, Lover, etc.)*
4. *Condemning, Judging, Criticizing, Righteous and Moralistic to Others*

Our Child Responds With Either Rebellion or Collapse

It is helpful to see that in response to an attack from this "Pusher-Judge," there is an inner dynamic set into motion. We both collapse and sink into shame and shock or we rebel and put up a fight. This dynamic has been there since early childhood. Some of us, because of our nature, may have reacted predominately with collapse and resignation. Others of us are more of the rebellious type. In either case, we are still under the thumb of the judge. It is still running the show and we react like puppets.

Anita, a participant in a workshop, was coming very late to every session. When we asked her why this was happening, she said that as a child, her mother was always rushing her. Now, she is late for everything. We told her that she could continue to come later if she liked. But as an experiment, she could also make a commitment to come on time and see what came up for her. After the second day, she began to feel a strong rage inside of her for always having been pushed in her life. It was important for her to connect with this rage because it has given her the fire to break from the negative forces of her repression. Prior to that, she was only expressing her anger indirectly in her chronic tardiness.

Anna Lisa, a young girl from the same workshop, lives with her mother and is in shame and shock most of the time. But she rebels by forgetting to do the things that her mother asks her to do. Anita picked the rebellious reaction while Anna Lisa has picked the collapsed one but behind both are the same feelings of rage and helplessness and it has been important for both of them to connect with their anger.

Beatrice, a woman in her early thirties, has been fighting all of her life. She cannot imagine what it would be like to not fight. It would be highly unusual for her to be collapsed because she doesn't allow it to happen. But since she is so strongly identified with her rebel, it is difficult for her to allow vulnerability and feel her fear. For someone like Beatrice who is familiar with playing the rebel, allowing herself to feel the collapse can be a doorway into her vulnerability.

However, we have strongly identified with our shame and shock and the collapse that goes with it, it may be more creative to explore the energy of the rebel. It takes much courage to move there because the fears of punishment or annihilation are so powerful if we disobey. Often when we are first becoming acquainted with our rebel, we can get over-whelmed with fear and guilt and run back again to our familiar collapse. Then we gather courage again and take another step into the rebel. While we are yet home as long as we are still rebelling against the judge, it is generally a more healthy reaction than collapsing because it has energy. And energy allows us to grow and break out of tyranny of the "Pusher-Judge."

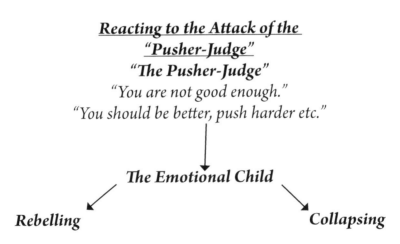

Reacting to the Attack of the "Pusher-Judge"

"The Pusher-Judge"
"You are not good enough."
"You should be better, push harder etc."

The Emotional Child

Rebelling   *Collapsing*

"Don't tell me what to do!"   "You are right, I should
try harder, "You can just go to hell!"   be and do better!"

We can notice the impact of our "Pusher-Judge" both in the ways we feel victimized and in the ways that we victimize others. With some people, we may be the "Pusher-Judge," with others we are the emotional children being pushed and judged. When we feel strong and important, we can heap abuse, impatience, frustration, criticism and demands on another. And we naturally put the same pressure and criticisms on ourselves.

I can see this in operation when I play tennis. If I miss a few shots, a voice comes out, "Krish, get the ball in! Get under the ball! Don't hit the ball so late! Move!" and so on. In these moments, I can have no doubt that this "Pusher-Judge" is always inside my head and I can start to feel myself shrinking under the self-criticism.

Making Our Own Rules
I have always set very high standards for myself that of course I could never live up to. And before I brought all of this into some awareness, I would place the same "very high standards" on everyone else and put them through the same torture that I was continually putting myself through. It still happens but I can catch it earlier because I can usually feel the pain it causes. When we put ourselves or others under the attack of the "Pusher-Judge;" it is deeply shaming and our emotional child goes in shock under the pressure.

When we believe that the "Pusher-Judge" is the voice of God, it is hard to tell that this complex is just a result of negative conditioning. When I first started to see that my "Pusher-Judge" was a liar, it was shattering. It was so much easier just to accept all these standards as the truth. It was just how life "should be". There was much security in simply accepting the Pusher-Judge as the voice of truth. I didn't have to question anything. I was basically living my life successfully obeying its commands.

> *I had built very effective compensations and I believed that my life "worked" if I followed them. In my case, it meant being a doctor who devoted my life to serving others, who did not indulge too much in material things, who kept busy learning and improving himself, who was not arrogant, selfish or pretentious and who was kind and sensitive to others. If I followed these dictates, I would become a "mensch" (which in Yiddish means a man of soul and depth). Who could argue with those values? Problem was they were given to me with the strong message that this is the only way to live.*
> *We have to learn to find our own standards and values.*

There are many ways to compensate. We can perform, try to impress, or strive for power and control. We can cultivate and get identified with roles, which make us feel good about ourselves. Then we cling to these roles and don't have to feel our shame underneath. All of these compensations are deeply unconscious mechanisms originating in childhood - the ways our child learned to cope with the "Pusher-Judge". It produces such stress inside that it is little wonder that we easily become exhausted, addictive or depressed.

There is a book that we both love very much - *The Education of Little Tree* by Forest Carter. It shows how a child can be brought up in a way where he learns to develop his own ways of living.

He receives guidance, support, direction, and even punishment but it is done in such a loving and permissive way that Little Tree grows up with a core of self-love and trust for his own judgment and capabilities. Without this inner trust and love, we grow up learning to compensate and compromise to meet the standards imposed upon us. We learn to listen to others and not to ourselves. We grow up a as slave to our "Pusher-Judge."

With a little understanding of psychology, we can have compassion for ourselves for being so dominated by this aggressive and repressive critic inside. As a child, we need and long for guidance. We cannot find our way in the world without it. Naturally, the guidance we receive comes from the "big people". Often with the very best of intentions, they impose their standards and values on us. The freer and more flexible standards and values we get and the more we will be taught to trust our own intelligence.

> *To develop a healthy guiding inner voice, what we call, "the inner wisdom", we need flexible rules, reasonable standards that are in tune with who we are as individuals, values that are based on love, firm but loving limits, and constant encouragement to learn to trust ourselves. Few of us got that. But we can begin to give that to ourselves.*

It is only once we discover and develop confidence in our own rules, standards and values that the tyranny of the "Pusher-Judge" begins to end. We begin by systematically and precisely questioning what we believe in to see if it is inherited or true to our nature. It is a process that continues until we feel enough inner strength and confidence to trust ourselves. Then we are out of the dynamic.

When we begin to work with this phenomenon, we start to realize how much we have struggled. We start to see how much we have had to leave ourselves to get the love and attention we needed to survive. And we start to see how profoundly it has run our lives. By bringing this dynamic into awareness, we can begin to recognize that the "Pusher-Judge" is a liar. It carries the harsh negative conditioning from our upbringing and knows nothing about who we are.

Here are some simple steps to get free of the "Pusher-Judge":

1. *Recognizing the Attack:* This involves recognizing each time we come under attack from the "Pusher-Judge" and learning to identify the triggers - the particular people and situations, statements and behavior that bring it on.

2. *Feeling the Attack:* Here, we learn to feel the impact of the attack - how we feel inside when it comes, what it does to our energy and what we think about ourselves when we are being pushed and judged. This basically means feeling the shame.

3. *Identifying The Roots of the Attack:* This aspect involves coming to understand more about the origin of our own "Pusher-Judge" - how our conditioning formed it. We can notice how, when we feel attacked, it relates back to former experiences in our life – principally the repressive, life-negative, pressuring, comparing, critical influences in our childhood that may have been direct or indirect. And this also involves becoming clearer what the voices are saying to us.

4. *Replace the "Pusher-Judge" with the "Inner Wisdom":* Whenever we feel under attack, we can choose to replace the voice or feeling of the "Pusher-Judge" with an "Inner Guide." The Guide comes with energy of loving support that is based on compassion and understanding of our own individual strengths and weaknesses. Sometimes, it can give us a "Zen hit" to wake us up from slumber, to encourage us to go for our vision in life or to remind us to live according to our heart and to our sensitivity, but the energy comes from love and support.

> *"People have judged you,*
> *And you have accepted their idea without scrutiny.*
> *You are suffering from all kinds of peoples' judgments*
> *And you are throwing those judgments on other people.*
> *If you want to get out of it,*
> *The first thing is: Don't judge yourself.*
> *Accept humbly your imperfections,*
> *Your failures, your mistakes, your frailties.*
> *It is just human."*
> Osho

Exercises: Bringing Light to Our Pusher-Judge
1. Begin to bring awareness to the times that you feel bad about yourself. Notice what triggered you to feel this way.
    a. What particular people bring on the attack and if so, what is it about these people that does it? Do you compare yourself unfavorably to them? What judgment or criticism do you feel?
    b. What specific situations bring on this attack? Is it when you feel pressured? Expected upon? Do you feel overwhelmed or intimidated?
    c. Does the criticism, blame or judgment come from outside or from inside you?

d. How do you feel when you come under attack? Pay attention to the specific body sensations that accompany an attack from your "Pusher-Judge".
   e. What are the voices saying to you when your inner child comes under attack?
2. When you notice yourself under attack from your "Pusher-Judge," what specific memories do you have from childhood?
   f. What situations do you remember that were similar?
   g. Who was it that was pushing or judging you - parent, teacher, anyone else?
   h. What was the verbal or nonverbal message that you were receiving at this time?
   i. What did you begin believing about yourself as a result of this attack?
3. When you are under an attack, how do you respond? Notice when and how you collapse. Notice when and how you compensate.
4. Draw a picture representing your "Pusher-Judge". Write what it is saying to you. Ask yourself if what it is saying is true. Notice at times you may be totally identified with your emotional child believing that the "Pusher Judge" is totally correct in what it says and feeling that you are totally taken over by the attack. Other times, you may have more distance. Notice this as if you were observing someone else.
5. Now draw a picture of your "Inner Guide". Write down what this energy is saying to you.

Chapter 14:

SHOCK

When I was in high school, I played second base for our school softball team. I was a good fielder and a very good hitter - in practice. But in regular season games, 1 struck out almost every time I came to bat and fumbled balls that I could have handled easily. The same would happen in tennis matches when we played against other schools. The greater the pressure, the more I fell apart. Something inside of me just stopped working. And there was nothing that I could do about it. I was stunned to discover much later that what 1 was experiencing was shock.

Shock is another of the significant landmarks of the inner landscape of the emotional child. It comes from a feeling of such profound fear that we disconnect and often cannot even feel, think, move or talk. It can arise unpredictably and suddenly in our life in any situation where there is the slightest bit of pressure, aggression or pain. This triggers an unconscious early trauma and we become dysfunctional. Shock has the power to cripple our ability to function normally in any aspect of our life.

Shock comes from trauma, usually repetitive trauma. Peter Levine, in his book, *Awakening the Tiger*, has a profound discussion for the dynamics of shock. He explains that the best way to understand shock is to imagine a small animal trapped in a corner by a predator - nowhere to hide, nowhere to escape to and unable to fight back because it is too small.

As a child, we were like that small animal. Our nervous system, built for fight or flight, had neither of these options available to it in situations when we felt trapped. It responded by freezing and the body's energy systems shut down. As a child when we experienced a trauma of any kind, we *were* trapped. These traumatic experiences occurred to us over and over again in some form. The result is a profound state of frozenness lurking inside that can be provoked at any time. This is shock. Even if we took ourselves away energetically from the threatening situation (called dissociating), our physiology still went into shock and we stored the painful memories in our unconscious.

Sometimes these repetitive traumas occurred so early or they were so subtle that we are not even aware that they occurred. An innocent, open, exquisitely sensitive infant or young child feels everything in his or her environment and is traumatized by the slightest violent or invasive energy or the slightest tension or unconsciousness in his or her surroundings. We were born into a society whose repressive and competitive values and nature was omnipresent.

If we consider the ways we were delivered, the way many of our parents related to each other, the life-style that either of them led, the ways that we were touched or the behaviors we witnessed in school, we may begin to appreciate the countess ways that we were traumatized. And add to this, the abuses, pressures, criticisms, and invasions that we may have received in childhood, we can begin to form a picture of our being shocked.

Today, when we experience something that resembles our early traumas, the shock arises. A participant once shared with us a charming story that is a good example of how shock comes up in our daily life. He has a strong controlling wife who, among other things, forbade him to eat in their fancy car because she didn't want to spoil the upholstery. One day, while they were driving in the German countryside, he bought some fresh cherries and started eating them in the car as they continued driving. She started to nag him but he told her that there was no problem since he was keeping all the pits in his mouth. At a certain point, he leaned over and spat them all out of the window. The only problem was that he forgot to lower the window. That's what happens in shock. We are so frightened that we do or say the stupidest things.

I used to have an aunt who gave new meaning to the word, "uptight". I now know that it was coming from her trauma but when I was a child when visiting her, all I knew was that I was tense as soon as I entered her house. And without exception, I would break something.

Many things can put us in shock. We call them *shock triggers*.

A shock trigger can be any kind of spoken or unspoken anger or violence, pressure, criticism, or judgment. It can be feeling controlled, manipulated or expected upon. It can be tension or negativity in the air or mixed messages. Even the threat of any of these can be enough. The slightest glance, the way someone speaks to us or doesn't speak to us, the inflection in a person's voice can be enough to trigger our shock.

Shock symptoms vary from one person to another.

We can get cold sweats, palpitations, extreme restlessness, or confusion. Some of us can be in some form of shock all the time. This can show itself as phobias, panic attacks, chronic restlessness, learning disorders or as chronic illness of some kind. We may try to compensate for it by spacing out and fantasizing but the experience remains in the body. I have a close friend who is brilliant. But his handwriting looks like that of a five year old. When he learned about shock, he understood why during most of his childhood, he was dyslexic.

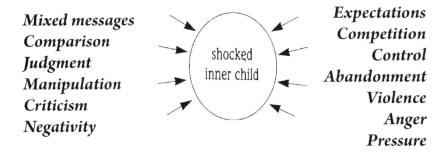

As with shame, we can have *shock related to different areas of our life.*

Shock can make us dysfunctional related to sex, feelings, anger and creativity. It is difficult to understand why shock comes in these significant areas of our lives. With shame, we may be able to identify the judgments we feel from ourselves or from others. But with shock, it is often a mystery. I have never been able to get clear where my shock came from. Probably from memories of trauma which are deeply unconscious. We can be making love and suddenly discover that we have gone away or our body stops responding. We may have difficulty feeling emotions we don't know why. Anger and confrontation or presenting ourselves in some way can create tremendous panic

Main Ways That Shock Shows Itself
1. *Sexual problems - unexplained fears, performance anxiety, premature ejaculation, impotence, inability to experience orgasm, pain in the genitals.*
2. *Fear of confrontation, anger, punishment or criticism*
3. *Difficulties with self-expression and creativity*
4. *Frozen feelings or lack of joy and enthusiasm*
5. *Confusion in thinking, planning or being present*
6. *Fears of intimacy or any social contact and isolation*
7. *Difficulty to take risks; panic in new situations or surroundings*

In the past, I believed that dysfunction and shock only came as a result of extreme and obvious trauma. But it isn't so. Situations that appear to us to be minor such as being controlled or manipulated to our emotional child were just as traumatic and shock producing. They can provoke as deep a shock as obvious cases of sexual or physical abuse. This understanding was important for me because it helped me to become more compassionate with myself. Also, we see it all the time in our work.

I also have noticed that just as with shame, when we have been shocked, we become identified with our shocked child and it causes us to become victimized in our relationships with people and with the world. Unconsciously, we see and feel ourselves as someone to be abused and as someone who deserves to be abused. This identification causes us to attract people who will treat us in similar ways that we were originally mistreated.

Once we understand this, it helps us to explain why we keep repeating the same traumatic experiences. I noticed that in the past, I would find myself with people who were more expressive and emotional than me and their expressiveness triggered my shock. Or I attracted people who triggered my shock because I felt controlled, manipulated, pressured or criticized. I would make very creative resolutions not to do it again. And then when I saw that nothing worked, I stopped just short of banging my head against a wall in frustration. But as the identification faded, so did the behavior.

When our shock is provoked, there is nothing to do but recognize it, feel it and validate it. Normally, we judge ourselves for our shock. Feeling helpless and paralyzed is probably not very high on our "things to be" list. We shame ourselves for being in shock and our shock becomes even worse. Giving space to allow our fears and our shock just to be is one of the most courageous and important steps we can take. In our work, when we guide people into exercises to connect more deeply with their state of shock, many times people tell us, "During the exercise, I didn't feel anything." Or, "Nothing happened for me." Our explanation is always similar. That's how shock is, we *don't feel anything* and it seems like *nothing is happening*. But if we can stay present to what *is* happening, we can begin to detect the frozenness – the frozenness of our feelings and our body.

Trying to push ourselves in some way to come out of shock only makes it worse. I have found, as with shame, that just knowing about shock - how it feels, what triggers it and where it comes from - has been enough to get distance from it and to watch it. This understanding slowly allowed me to be able to be with it without so much judgment and gradually to begin remembering that when my emotional child goes into shock, it is not who I am.

CHAPTER 14: SHOCK

> *"This is the greatest crime that society*
> *Commits against every child.*
> *No other crime can be worse than this.*
> *To destroy a child's trust is to spoil his whole life*
> *Because trust is so valuable that the moment you lose trust,*
> *You also lose your contact with your own being."*
> Osho

Exercises:
(Exploring shock is a delicate matter and usually requires help from a professional. These exercises can just be a guide to understand your shock more deeply.)

1. The Experience of Shock

a) How would you describe your own shock experience? What happens in the body? Speediness? Restlessness? Sweating? Confusion? Paralysis? Inability to feel? Inability to speak?

b) In what areas of your life do you feel shock? Sex? Feelings? Anger or Confrontation? Intimacy? Creativity? How do you feel it in these areas?

2. Identifying the Shock Triggers

Pick a few of the last times you experienced shock. What brings on your shock? Pressure? Anger? Aggression? Criticism? Fear of or the experience of being left or rejected? Not getting the attention you want? Someone being out of control, hysterical, illogical, or demanding?

3. The Origin of Shock

Some of us have a good idea of how we were shocked as a child. But for some of us, it is a mystery. What picture do you have for how you might have been shocked? What frightened you and what created disturbance? (Remember, the smallest things can terrify a child.) It can help to imagine a child who is not you growing up in the environment in which you were raised. What would he or she feel? Would he or she feel safe? How was it for this child to feel feelings? To give and receive anger? To be direct and open? To be sad or afraid? How was he or she supported or not supported in being creative? How was he or she pressured?

Chapter 15:

ABANDONMENT, DEPRIVATION, AND NEGLECT

A friend of mine had been in a relationship for seven years. During that time, she often complained that she was not getting enough space and that her boyfriend's emotional needs were too overwhelming. She also felt that he was not enough "in his energy" to meet her own needs - particularly in sex. Over the years, he had had occasional lovers but it was more a strategy to escape her nagging than anything else. About a year ago, she fell in love with someone and had a short affair. She knew it was mostly just to get even. But it seemed to be the final blow for her long-term relationship. They fought more and more and finally split up.

The breakup put my friend into a deep process that brought up more pain and loneliness than she ever felt before. Now, she looks back at the whole experience, including the time it has taken for her to recover with much gratitude. It opened up a wound inside of her that she had skillfully avoided feeling all of her life. Once the trauma of the breakup subsided, she felt that a whole new world of sensitivity and inner awareness had opened up for her.

When we enter into our own inner world of abandonment, and deprivation, neglect, we are entering into a world of a very small child who is desperate for love, who feels lonely, frightened and unprotected and who longs for someone to take care of him or her. This inner space contains such intense panic that often we can spend much of our life avoiding it. However when someone leaves us or when we feel isolated and lonely, this place opens up. Seen through the eyes of our emotional child, we believe that no one will ever be there for us. Our behavior in relationships - our jealousy, our avoidance of intimacy, our panic that the other will leave us, our wanting and demanding more from the other person - reflects this deep belief. When we have been left, the place of *abandonment* opens in its fullest extent.

But in all the ways that we feel lonely, unloved, not respected, uncared for, and unseen, the abandonment wound is exposed in smaller doses. This is *deprivation or neglect,* simply another face of abandonment. This wound affects our relating more than any other. The fear of abandonment provokes extreme terror because as a child, we had countless experiences that left us feeling that our survival was threatened. Many of these experiences are not conscious because we covered them up. However, when something happens in our life today that unconsciously reminds us of this experience, we feel that we are going to die. Inside, we are in total panic.

> *The wound of abandonment opens when we experience a loss. Deprivation is a small dose of the abandonment wound that gets triggered whenever an expectation if not met.*

But often, we are not in touch with the depth and intensity of this fear until we go through a deep abandonment experience. I had not a clue that this place existed until I broke up with the first major love of my life, a woman whom I had been with during my last two years in university. Prior to that, I was merrily going along with my life, obsessed with my career and with sports and on the whole living in a way that was very unconscious of the deeper aspects of life.

When we split up, I was in such pain that I did not know if I could make it from one day to the next. And it made no sense because we both knew that the relationship was over and we had to go our own ways. I had no idea where all this pain was coming from. It lasted for two years. I didn't know that I was touching a primal wound. I didn't even know what "primal" meant in those days. But since, I have discovered deeper and deeper layers of this wound. In a sense, all my subsequent significant relationships have taken me on another step toward accepting the profound loneliness that I have held inside.

Abandonment and Deprivation Come From Our Inner Emptiness

The wound arises out of a memory (and experience) of not receiving the nourishment we needed. This memory is not so much a recollection of a specific event or events as it is a cellular experience of negative emptiness that our emotional child is desperate to fill. The pain of the wound lies under the surface. When we have not consciously chosen to embrace it, we automatically and compulsively move into compensations or addictions to avoid feeling it. We can become cool, distant, and anti-dependent or painfully clingy and dependent.

I have been down both of these roads. I was married for five years to a woman who suffered from severe depression. I could not understand why she was not able to just "kick herself out of it" and I felt helpless to do anything to help her. I could not grasp what she was going through because I simply had not touched the same level of depth that she had. I was comfortable in my anti-dependency. It was safer not to need and also not to have to feel any pain or fear.

Years after that, as so often happens, I swung to the other extreme and was with women who needed and wanted me less than I needed or wanted them. I got a bit of my own medicine back, feeling rejected and needy instead of confident and "together". These are some of the ways that we play out our abandonment wound in our relating when we have not deeply explored it. We act it out in our jealousy dramas, our avoidance of intimacy, and in our demands and expectations on our lover and friends. One way of another, we are compensating for the terrifying fear of being left.

Our compensations can become painfully compulsive and addictive. For instance, recently a woman came to see us with a story of a destructive relationship with a man. She kept going back to him even though he was continually rejecting her. The more he rejected her, the more she begged. We asked her what keeps her going back. Her answer was that after two weeks without him, she feels so much anxiety that she can't help herself. She knows that it isn't love but just the thought of making love again with him is enough to want to see him.

Most of the time, when two people come together, under the surface of the courting game and the whole energy bazaar, are two starving emotional children each unconsciously expecting or hoping that the other person will fill their hole. Even the most hardcore anti-dependent has an emotional child lurking inside full of unmet needs and expectations.

> *Our unmet needs have remained on the back burner of our awareness waiting for the right person and the right situation to bring them out. They don't go away, they only go into denial.*

Intimacy Brings Up Our Abandonment Wound

But intimacy brings them all up. We may have no clue how needy and starving we are until we take the risk to open deeply to someone. A client of ours had history of being in relationships and at the same time, having affairs on the side. He felt that this was a healthy way to be in relationship because it kept things alive. When we suggested to him that perhaps he could be so cavalier only because he had yet to be truly in love, he objected vehemently. But a year after we said this, he did enter into a deep love with a woman. All of a sudden, his desire to sleep with other women vanished and he was allowing himself to connect with his neediness and insecurity.

Our demands and expectations can come out in sex, in communication, in time spent together, in being seen and understood, in being provided for financially, in any way that could fill our hole inside.

> *We expect and demand because we feel deprived and neglected but these expectations and demands only lead to more deprivation. When we expect, we cannot receive.*

Dysfunction Arises When We Don't Face This Emptiness

Since no one can possibly fulfill our demands, our relating can become dominated by conflict and frustration. We use all kinds of strategies to fill the hole rather than feel the emptiness. For instance, we play the role of a good father to make someone dependent on us all the time believing that we are just being caring. Or we play the role of the attentive mother but actually we are simply covering up our own fears of being left. We play the game of being seductive and charming but never risk a deeply committed relationship because of our fears of rejection. We may enter into relationship but always keep a back door open in subtle and perhaps not so subtle ways.

To make matters more complicated, often our expectations and needs collide. A couple we worked with a while ago fought because she wanted him to make long term commitments while he felt that long term commitments would jeopardize his freedom. Her longing for security and commitment conflicted with his not wanting to imprison himself with obligations. In the past, he had always given up his own needs. He was willing to be emotionally present and committed without tying himself to future plans while he learned to honor his own needs for individuation. But she could not feel safe with so little security.

This conflict strongly brought up both of their abandonment wounds. For him to stand by his needs to find himself brought up the terror that she would leave and for her not to have clear future plans brought up tremendous panic. But fortunately, they both had the courage and commitment to their growth to focus on feeling their wound rather than compensating with compromise (his case) and demands (hers).

These are all covers for our abandonment fears. When someone is not how we want him or her to be - not there for us, not giving us what we feel we need, not understanding, we feel lonely. Even the smallest things that another does can make us feel that he or she is not there for us. In an instant, all our feelings of togetherness and of companionship are gone. We are flooded with fear and with the speed of light, we move into a reaction – to compromise, to fight, cut off, blame, attack, please - anything to make the uncomfortable feeling go away.

The panic of loneliness is so strong and so compelling that it compels us to react. We are in a fully automatic, habitual, and compulsive mode. And just to make matters worse, we are drawn to come close to people who in some way will trigger our unhealed wound of abandonment. Existence seems to want us to face this wound. In a line-up of five possible people, four of whom would give us everything that we think we want, we always seem to pick the one person who will push our abandonment buttons.

Anger, Rage and Resentment is Part of the Wound
The dark side of the abandonment wound is the profound anger we carry inside for feeling betrayed. Most of us carry rage with the opposite sex based on memories of betrayal going back to our mothers or fathers. But it is generally unconscious and only comes up after we have been together with someone for a while. While deep down we want to give and receive love, what is often on the surface is the desire for revenge. Our anger gets reawakened slowly and steadily in all the little and big ways that we feel let down by our lovers and friends.

For example, in a recent session, a man was telling me that his girlfriend had made love to his best friend. When I asked him what was going on in the relationship prior to this, he shared with me that he had felt deprived in sex because he felt she was "too spiritual" and he was having fantasies of others. As we explored more deeply, it came out that he was re-enacting in very similar ways the dynamic that he had had with his mother in relation to sex. She had made him promise to become a "nice" man and not to follow the footsteps of his "sexually obsessed" father. Naturally, he was storing a great deal of unconscious rage for allowing his mother to castrate his energy in such a way. Slowly he could see how much rage he had toward women.

Our unconscious rage reactions on each other are not very helpful. Before we can do any significant work, we have to make a commitment not to throw our anger on the other. It is helpful to start working with our anger in ways that are not destructive. Otherwise we will leak our anger unconsciously. In our experience, when we have not worked constructively with our anger, for instance in individual therapy that creates space for expression or workshops that provide structures to experience anger, we will throw it on each other in all kinds of destructive ways. One couple we worked with would repeatedly attack and accuse each other in the name of "sharing".

> *"Sharing" before we have developed deep understanding for our abandonment wound often is motivated by a need for recognition, love, or attention or the compulsion to blame and accuse, and be right.*

Between the Trigger and the Reaction Lies the Wound

Unknowingly, we are looking for an opportunity to justify our anger and mistrust and take revenge or react. When something triggers our abandonment wound, we move from trigger to reaction without even a millisecond gap. The mechanism is immediate and deeply automatic. One device that we work with is attempting to stretch the time frame between trigger and reaction so that there is time and space to feel and be with the wound when it is being provoked. We lengthen the distance between these two events to create time to feel. The wound is always there but normally we don't have time to feel it because we move so quickly into reaction.

Between Trigger and Reaction Lies the Wound

Trigger	→	*(the Wound)* →	*Reaction*
E.g. Rejection, loss, unmet expectations, invasions		*Fear, emptiness, hopelessness, helplessness and pain.*	*e.g. Anger, blame, withdrawal, collapse, manipulation, control, addictions, resignation*

Before we understand about our abandonment, it is difficult not to react or be addicted. Trying to stop these with our will power only makes us uptight and judge ourselves because we always fall back. The fears behind our abandonment are so strong that it even overpowers our will. But as we begin to appreciate the depth and intensity of the abandonment panic, we begin to see how profoundly these forces affect our relating. This understanding gradually gives us space from our compulsive and mechanical reactions.

We bring awareness to our wound of abandonment by paying attention to the big and the little moments that provoke it.

The big moments such as rejection, loss, or the end of a relationship usually get our attention because they are so painful. But often we get lost in the fears and there is no one who is watching. We are terrified and the loss or rejection only strengthens our mistrust and resignation. As we begin to watch with more understanding, we can begin to see that the wound has been triggered, that it has always been there and that we get stronger by the process of grief.

The little moments would normally pass by without our even recognizing that the abandonment wound has been triggered. These are the times when we get irritated or angry when things don't go our way, the moments when an expectation is not met, and the moments when we feel deprived of love, attention, respect, sensitivity or touch. In these times, we move quickly into a reaction (which often elicits reaction in return) or into an addiction.

Some Situations Provoke Overwhelming Abandonment

The situation of being in a love triangle is important to mention when we talk about abandonment. When a person is on a leg of a triangle and his or her lover is also involved with someone else, it is a continual provocation of the wound. It is like being on intravenous abandonment. That does not mean that we can or should avoid these situations. Sometimes it is what life brings and what we need to experience for some reason. But it can also be masochistic and re-enacting our shame and abandonment from childhood. The same can be true when we are together with someone who is unavailable.

Sometimes, out of our shame and past experience of feeling unloved, we find ourselves in a relationship in which there is really no nourishment at all. If we evaluate a relationship that we are in and conclude, *from a rational and balanced space,* that there is truly not enough nourishment and it is repeating a destructive pattern, it is time to leave.

Madeleine in a workshop was sharing that she was unhappy in her life with her husband of fifteen years.

"He comes home from work and moves directly into watching TV. We seldom spend time together and when we do, all we talk about is practical stuff about our life and the children."

"Are you open to doing couples' counseling?" We asked.

"Yes, totally. But he doesn't want. He just says that it's me trying to control him. It's true that I nag at him but it's because I am so unhappy."

"What keeps you together?" We asked.

"I keep thinking that it will get better. But if I am honest, I think that I am afraid of being alone."

"It seems that you have to reach a point where you can say to him that it is absolutely crucial that we work on this because I can't live like this any longer. And be willing to risk that it will be the end of the relationship."

"Yes, I can see that, but I am not ready yet."

"That's totally fine, but meanwhile, it is important that you feel the price you pay by not taking it to the limit."

Facing Our Abandonment Wound Paves the Way for Real Love

Loss and disappointment are experiences that we all have to go through in life. When we are more able to watch, we can receive these periods in our life, feel the pain, however profound and continue on with our lives. If we are able to stay with the experience of fear and pain that comes whenever it gets triggered, it heals and we develop more and more space for each new trigger. By riding through the fears and the pain when it comes, we slowly become less controlled by our child state of mind. Our emotional child has less and less impact on how we see and feel the experiences that are happening in our present life and our perceptions become less contaminated with past traumas.

Working through the abandonment wound is the basic ingredient in being able to create love. One aspect, for sure, is being aware that it is there. Another is feeling it and knowing a bit about where it comes from. Also, when we go through this process, we reach certain understandings that seem essential for being with someone.

One is that people are how they are and we cannot expect them to change. Another is that there will be times when my emotional child will feel neglected and deprived because there will always be aspects of the other's personality which I won't like. When we encounter them, we may feel very alone, frustrated and disappointed.

Also, in every relationship, there are going to be times when both persons are not getting what they think they need. And finally, if we open deeply to someone, we have to be willing to face the possibility that we will lose that person one way or another.

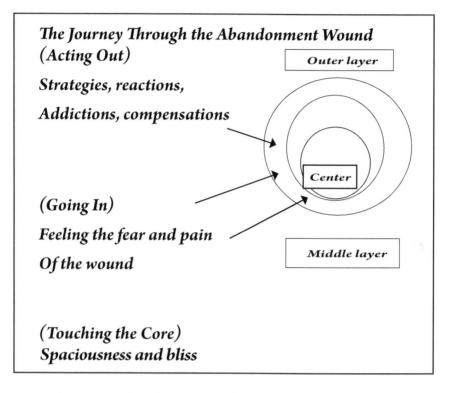

Osho, our teacher, describes a big difference between loneliness and aloneness. Loneliness is a dark hole, a frightening negative space. But aloneness is our nature; what he describes as the Everest of meditation. Prior to exploring my own abandonment wound, I had no idea what he was talking about.

Now I can see that my feelings of emptiness are the way my emotional child feels and thinks and will probably always think. This mind set can be provoked at any time, but I have had enough positive experiences of aloneness to know that this feeling of loneliness passes. Aloneness, in my experience, can be extremely blissful and it can be bitter sweet, but it does not have the panic, or the desperation that loneliness has. It is just how life is.

However, with the first attack of our abandonment wound, what we experience is the panic of loneliness. It takes accepting and allowing these feelings inside for the space of aloneness to open to us.

> *"You have to encounter your emptiness.*
> *You have to live it, you have to accept it.*
> *And in your acceptance is hidden a great revelation.*
> *The moment you accept your aloneness,*
> *your emptiness,*
> *Its very quality changes.*
> *It becomes just its opposite –*
> *It becomes an abundance, a fulfillment,*
> *An overflowing of love and joy."*
> Osho

Exercises:
1. Bringing Awareness to Your Wound of Neglect and Deprivation.

Answer the question, "I feel deprived and neglected (hurt or angry) when..."

    a. What specific behavior makes you feel betrayed or deprived in your intimate relationships? Specifically, what is it that the person does or does not do, says or does not say?
    b. What expectations do you have in these cases?
    c. What beliefs do you have related to these situations?

2. Tracing the Wound to Its Source.
    a. In what ways did you feel deprived, neglected, or abandoned in similar ways as a child? Feeling that no one was there? Feeling invaded? Feeling misunderstood? Feeling no one listened or ignored?
    b. How did you learn to cope with this neglect? What beliefs did you form about life as result?

3. Feeling the Wound

The next time you find yourself triggered in neglect or deprivation, practice taking the energy away from reaction and just going in and feeling what is happening inside.
    a. What does it feel like in the body?
    b. What thoughts come up? What are your fears?
    c. What does your energy want to do?

Chapter 16:

ENGULFMENT

In our workshops, we generally have more women than men. Part of the reason, we suppose, is that women are more inclined to recognize that intimacy and co-dependency are issues that they need to work on. Another reason is that many men have a deep wound of engulfment and they are extremely wary of exposure or of allowing themselves to be vulnerable in unfamiliar situations. When our emotional child has been engulfed, we are suspicious of letting anyone come close and we are even suspicious of being vulnerable. Although it is usually unconscious, our past experience with "love" is associated with pain and betrayal, with being possessed, repressed, manipulated or controlled.

Engulfment is the twin wound of abandonment and just as powerful. Sometimes, depending on our childhood conditioning, we are more in touch with our fears of being controlled, manipulated, or possessed than we are of being left. The engulfment fear can be so strong that we effectively avoid allowing anyone to come close or if we do, we are continually in dread of being overpowered. I have found that this fear is even accompanied with feelings of being hot, not being able to breath or claustrophobia. As in the case with each of the wounds we have discussed, the feeling of engulfment can be triggered by the slightest and seemingly irrational provocation. And once triggered, there is often an overpowering feeling to get as far as possible away from the threat as soon as possible.

The Causes of Engulfment
There can be many psychological reasons that this wound is so strong. We could have had an overpowering and controlling parent, particularly of the opposite sex. Or we could have been an emotional substitute, providing for our mother or father the love or nourishment he or she was not getting from his or her spouse. Or for one reason or another, our mother or father may not have wanted us to grow up and become a sexual, powerful and independent person. But with this wound, as with every other one, it is not possible to explain all of its origin and power simply by tracing its childhood roots. Whatever the reason, we carry a feeling inside that "love" is not to be trusted.

To be engulfed is highly abusive because it damages our ability to learn how to master our universe. Without this ability, we cannot develop self-esteem. Therefore, for someone with a strong engulfment wound, he or she has a deep and powerful belief that his or her life energy, creativity, freedom, sexuality or even spirituality will be suppressed and destroyed once he allows someone to come close. This fear produces a powerful inner conflict.

We know that we cannot live without love yet we don't trust love. We initiate love and then push it away - over and over again. One part of us, that part which wants love, attracts it and may even begin a deepening relationship. Then, our emotional child who holds the engulfment wound reacts at the slightest indication of control, manipulation or possession. Our reactions are seldom related to reality and the other person feels unjustly treated. His or her efforts to come close to the engulfed person are continually met with frustration and disappointment. Often, the person doing the pushing away feels painfully guilty for his or her behavior, but the forces that are in operation here are so strong that it is pointless to try and control them.

If we recognize that we have a pattern of pushing people away or of avoiding intimacy, most likely it is because we are identified with our wound of engulfment. We may be able to trace the origin of this fear back to a particular childhood situation where "love" came with considerable control and repression leaving us with a profound feeling of betrayal. But it doesn't really matter how much we can trace back to our conditioning. What does matter is that as long as we are identified with our engulfment, we have no control over our feelings and behavior. They are uncontrollable, irrational and overpowering.

> *It is important to remember that when we feel engulfed in our current relationships, it is the tip of the iceberg. Perhaps our lover or friend is doing or saying something make provokes our feeling controlled, manipulated, or possessed but the root is in childhood.*

If we fall into the trap of believing that the other person is the problem, we will perpetuate the same dramas over and over again of coming close and then pulling away in righteous indignation. Or we will live a life of isolation because inside we believe that love only ends in control.

Acting Out from the Wound

In relationships, the person who has a strong engulfment wound usually acts it out by becoming anti-dependent. The anti-dependent is terrified of closeness because it puts him (or her) face to face with his original engulfment trauma that was a deep betrayal of love. He or she swings on a pendulum between being defiant and rebellious in his freedom and independence and then when feeling guilty or hungry for love, he or she moves over to being pleasing and compliant. Then he gets angry and feels constricted and swings back to his defiant, rebellious position. This swing doesn't lead to any shift in consciousness unless there is some awareness for what is going on underneath.

When our emotional child feels engulfed, we believe that the only

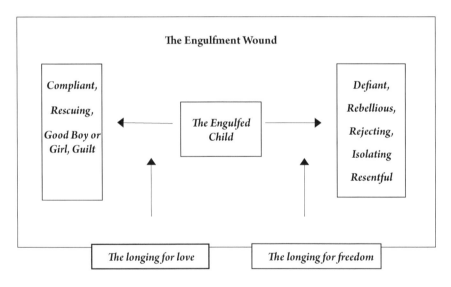

But the freedom we seek can never come from reacting to another person. His or her behavior toward us is not what is keeping us imprisoned. Our freedom is ours to take at any moment.

What keeps us imprisoned is that we live in reaction without any awareness of what or why we are behaving as we do. My engulfment wound could match anyone's in intensity. I will always remember that as a child, there was a huge marble sculpture that my mother made and had standing right outside the door of our house. It was a torso of a large buxom woman holding a little boy under her arm. Just the head of the little boy was peeping out from under this enormous arm. Once I asked my mother who the little boy was.

"Oh, that's you!" she answered, feeling very proud, protective, and motherly. Needless to say, I didn't the share the same unambiguous enthusiasm about this sculpture and what it portrayed as she did. Much later, in a particularly strong therapy session, I connected with how deeply bonded I had been to my mother. As an infant, I had malabsorption syndrome and nearly died. My mother sat by the crib in the hospital night and day for over a week willing me to live. Something must have happened during that time - a bond was formed. Also, my father was away working in Europe and I didn't even meet him until I was two years old. I discovered in that session how conflicted I had been between feeling my mother's love and caring on one hand and her over-protectiveness on the other that hindered me from finding my manhood.

Engulfment Creates Powerful Inner Conflict
The fear of losing the love of the mother and our longing for freedom can become a huge struggle if we open deeply to someone. As I explored what made it difficult for me to do what I wanted to do, I found that I came face to face with my emotional child's dread of punishment or rejection. Each time

I went against another person's expectations or demands, each time I disappointed someone I loved, I had to deal with this fear.

When we are identified with our engulfed emotional child, we have a very ambivalent relation to those we come close to. We often only have a vague sense of what we really want. We act out with a little acts of rebellion and then feel horribly guilty that we have hurt or betrayed the other person. We want love and we want freedom and we are hopelessly lost somewhere in the middle. We feel guilty whenever we take space and resentful when we don't. As a result, we have a hard time doing either. Rebelling against someone who puts demands and expectations on us is often the only way that we think we can reconnect with our own needs.

But this can easily become an automatic unconscious endless pattern of reacting. It has helped me to come out of my automatic reactions by letting myself feel the fears of being smothered when they are provoked, staying present, and even sharing what comes up. Normally I would react or keep myself chronically removed just to lessen the anxiety and fear. But by coming out of this automatic behavior and staying more present to the fears of closeness, I connected with the trust that was damaged and the grief of a child who opened and experienced his openness abused. I could appreciate why my vulnerability went into hiding.

Exploring this, I have felt a deep sorrow because I recognized how I had hurt others and myself because of the mistrust that I held inside. I saw how my acting out in rebellion and resentment had hurt those who tried to get close to me and how I held them responsible for wounds that were there long before they ever came into my life. I also recognized all the moments of missed intimacy with women I had been with, with friends and with family.

> *This is the pain of engulfment. It can shut us down emotionally so profoundly that it takes much trust, patience and self-acceptance to open again.*

Fortunately, with Amana, I have been able to open and expose myself in ways that I never thought possible. To help break out identification with the engulfed child, we also have to take risks to do what we want to do and feel the fear that it provokes. My normal behavior would be to deny myself the experiences I longed for because of the fear that that the other person would not like it. This was particularly strong for me in the past when it meant spending time with friends instead of with the woman I was with or doing anything which took time away from the relationship. It sounds absurd to me but I actually didn't think I had the right to take time for myself and do the things that I wanted to do.

Freedom Is Our Responsibility

That is the guilt that seems to go with engulfment. To take the risk was terrifying. As a result, I would do what I wanted to do but from a reactive and rebellious space, feeling angry, resentful and guilty. Naturally I would get a reaction back. Then I went into the trance that I was not "being given my space." It was my fears, not the other's expectations that were the problem. Once I gathered the strength to take these risks and take them with clarity rather than reaction, it became more and more clear that others' demands, expectations and reactions do not matter.

> *Once we get clear that we have the right to take our own space and are willing to face our fears if we do, the dance is over. The process is with ourselves, with our own fears, with learning and validating our own needs and wants, with finding the courage to risk.*

I remember an incident some years ago, not long after we started being together. We were in Denmark, where she comes from. I usually feel a bit insecure there - I don't speak the language, it is her home and she was among many old friends. We stopped to put gas in the car and she casually told me how to do it. Amana is precise and particular which I easy interpret as control and interference. I reacted with, "Just don't tell me what to do." At that moment, I realized that I was not talking to her. It was coming out of the past.

When we go to visit our family, particularly mother and father, it can be a good meditation on engulfment. As soon as we feel patronized, given advice to, told how to be, criticized or perhaps just receiving a comment about our life, we can easily regress into that small child again. They get lost in unconscious parenting, we get lost in unconscious "childing". Remembering the difference between the present and the past is a big part of dropping our identification with an engulfed child.

One last point strikes me as important to mention. When we have an engulfment wound, we have unspoken expectations that others should be sensitive, respectful, considerate and understanding. We want the world to match our ideals. And we get indignant and angry when people disappoint us. But people don't change to fit our expectations. They are how they are. Still, at the moment we feel someone has been disrespectful or possessive, we feel alone and betrayed. Our lesson in that moment is to set a limit. That's the skill we lost as a child because of course, a child cannot set limits. But now we can. So, when we are willing to face the aloneness, and gradually learn to stand up for ourselves, we heal the engulfment wound. As our confidence in setting limits deepens, our expectations slowly begin to drop away.

Healing the Engulfment Wound
a. *Feeling and validating the fears inside each time we feel engulfed.*
b. *Breaking the automatic pattern of pulling away or reacting by sharing the fears instead.*
c. *Separating the past from the present.*
d. *Noticing our expectations that people should be as we want them to be.*
e. *Risking validating and honoring our own needs and energy in spite of our guilt and our fears of rejection or punishment. That often requires learning to set firm but loving limits.*

> *"There is only one basic fear.*
> *The fear is of losing yourself.*
> *It may be death; it may be in love,*
> *But the fear is the same;*
> *You are afraid of losing yourself.*

*And the strangest thing is that
Only those people are afraid of losing
themselves
Who don't have themselves.
Those who have themselves are not afraid."*
Osho

Exercises: Working with the Wound of Engulfment
1. Notice the moments that you feel possessed, demanded upon, controlled or overwhelmed by someone. What are your beliefs at these moments about how people are toward you? Write them down. E.g. "I feel that this person (or people or life in general) are out for themselves." "I feel that my needs are never considered."
2. What feelings and body sensations do you have connected to your feeling engulfed, smothered and overwhelmed? Hot? Difficulty breathing? Panic? Urgency to get away and be alone?
3. In what specific ways do you feel you were demanded upon, possessed, controlled or overwhelmed as a child? Notice specific situations with specific people - e.g. mother, father or siblings. Is there any connection between these situations and those you observe in your life today?
4. Pick a specific situation where you feel or felt demanded or expected upon or smothered. What would you need to say if you stand up for what you need? What fears come up for you when you consider taking the "space" you need and doing what you want or setting a limit?

5. What are your expectations with those people with whom you feel engulfed, disrespected or disappointed by? Write them down - e.g." I feel that he or she should be more..."
6. What would it be like for you to let go of these expectations with this person? What fears would arise?

Chapter 17:

MISTRUST AND ANGER

There is a story of a samurai who went to visit a Zen master and asked him to tell him the difference between heaven and hell. The Zen master looked him over and told him that he didn't have any time to waste on a stupid man like him. The samurai became enraged and drawing his sword, threatened to strike the aged teacher. The Zen master stopped him and said, "That, sir, is hell." Immediately, the samurai was struck with the wisdom and power of the man. He sheathed his sword and bowed in respect. The master said, "And that, sir, is heaven."

Mistrust and the anger that surrounds it is the last stop on our tour of the inner world of the emotional child. Our mistrust is our hell. When we enter into our mistrust bubble, we are entering into a very dark space. In this bubble, we are imprisoned in our own negative beliefs, perceptions, and expectations. They shut out our ability to receive and appreciate love or beauty. Mistrust is also the easy way out because there is no risk. It is the way of the world and therefore, we can readily find support for our mistrustful beliefs and opinions. Moving into trust takes much courage.

I remember once as a child asking my mother what God was. She said to me that it was just an idea. My parents were both in rebellion to any kind of religion or spirituality. I always thought this was very intelligent of them and liberating for me since I was never indoctrinated with any traditional or conventional religious beliefs or practices. But there was also air of skepticism and rationality that came with the upbringing I received and I was taught that it is wiser to doubt and mistrust.

I missed to be taught to appreciate the mystery and magic in life. One of the reasons that I am so touched by *The Education of Little Tree* by Forest Carter, the book we referred to previously, is the way that Little Tree's grandparents imparted to him a deeply heartful spirituality full of respect and trust for life. This sense of basic trust does not leave him even though he goes through deeply traumatic experiences including physical abuse, loss and betrayal.

Living in Mistrust is Familial

Most of the time we live in mistrust. We can see the proof of how profound our mistrust is when we witness how easily it can be triggered. When someone does or says something that makes us feel disrespected, we feel betrayed and enter into a familiar world of resignation, isolation, separation, withdrawal, anger and hurt. This can also happen when we experience adverse life circumstances. We may have moments of trust but underneath, there is a core of mistrust inside.

If we had a core of trust, we would feel invasions or adverse life events as painful but quickly let them go. Instead, they register with a deep hurt place inside where we do not feel safe or cared for by life and people. Our natural innocence and trust in existence has been damaged and our emotional child looks out through eyes of caution and suspicion.

When triggered, every hurt and invasion that we ever received but were unable to feel and process comes up. We store every insult to our dignity and integrity inside as an inner resentment bank. When we experience a hurt in our life today, it triggers every hurt that we ever experienced. This is our mistrust bubble. Inside the bubble, our emotional child is guarded, protected and full of suspicion coming from a lifetime of hurts and infected with all the negative, mistrusting thought forms of those who raised us. We actually believe that what we see is the truth. We live in a perpetual state of dread that we will be violated or betrayed again as we were in the past. From this bubble, we expect the worst. We believe that we will never get what we need, never be understood, never be respected and always get invaded.

Recently, we saw a couple that came for a session because their life together had become a nightmare of drama. They had a four and a half year old child and wanted to preserve the family but they spent most of their time fighting. Not long into the session, it became clear that there was no trust between them. Each one had successfully triggered the other's deepest wounds. She felt unloved and unappreciated while he felt suffocated. They also began sleeping with other lovers. He was so mistrustful that he didn't even want to come to the session but he did realize that he was in a pattern that was repeating itself. Both could see that their mistrust started long before they had ever met each other.

> *Many couples we work with live in this kind of misery. The salvation comes when each person begins to see that his and her mistrust is not caused, but rather triggered, by the other person and begins to work with the underlying wound that his its roots in childhood.*

The Bridge Between Us and Others Broke Long Ago

Because of the invasions, neglect, and betrayals we sustained as a child, the bridge between us and others has been broken long ago. When we enter into relationships in our life today, any relationship, we are already in the mistrust bubble even though we may feel full of trust and hope. Most of the time, the trust we are feeling is not real. It is a fantasy of our magical (emotional) child. As soon as the other person does anything that feels invasive or disrespectful, we are back in our normal state of mistrust. Then we are fully convinced that all our misgivings about opening and trusting someone are validated. From the mistrust bubble, and through the eyes of our mistrusting emotional child, we believe that the other person is the problem. We believe that we could be open if the other person were just more sensitive or more available. From this place, we fully believe that we can trust only if another lives up to our expectations of how we should be treated.

In another session, a woman was sharing with us that she had just split from her boyfriend because he was "not considerate enough of her feelings". As we traced back to other experiences with men in the past, it became very clear that in one way or another, none of them could live up to her expectations. We asked her to step into the shoes of her ex-boyfriend for a moment and see what he felt relating to her. Tears came almost immediately. Speaking for him, she shared how much love he felt for her but felt helpless because he could not possibly live up to her expectations. Slowly she could see that her expectations were keeping her safe. It created a barrier between her and everyone she came close to by protecting her from having to feel vulnerable.

Let's look more precisely at how mistrust drives the mind of the emotional child:

a) Our original trust was damaged leaving us mistrustful of life and others and causing us unknowingly to retreat into our own world.
b) Now, instead of looking out through eyes of trust, our present vision is clouded with past experiences of invasion and betrayal. Deep inside, we expect them to happen again.
c) However, we have a longing for love. We also recognize somewhere deep inside that it is not healthy for us to remain closed in our safe, protected arid isolated world. We try opening to someone.
d) But our unexplored wounds cause us to repeat our story of invasion and betrayal. Because of our mistrust wound, we open with hidden expectations. We don't really open, we have an agenda for the other person to fulfill. We expect that he or she won't invade or betray us.

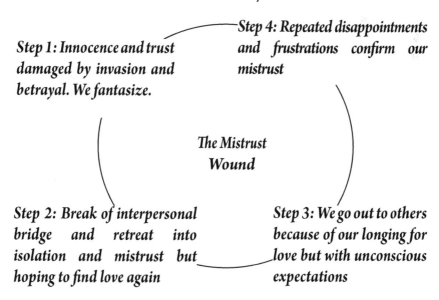

Step 1: Innocence and trust damaged by invasion and betrayal. We fantasize.

Step 4: Repeated disappointments and frustrations confirm our mistrust

The Mistrust Wound

Step 2: Break of interpersonal bridge and retreat into isolation and mistrust but hoping to find love again

Step 3: We go out to others because of our longing for love but with unconscious expectations

e) We have a certain grace period in which the other person still glows with our idealization. But as soon as we feel invaded or betrayed, we simply retreat back into our safe, isolated world feeling that our mistrusting beliefs have been validated. We end up where we started.

Coming Out of Mistrust

How can we come out of our mistrust bubble? Like all our bubbles - shame, abandonment, shock or engulfment, the first step is just being aware that we are in a mistrust bubble. The key for me is to remember when I am feeling mistrust; the incident is only a trigger of a much deeper mistrust that I carry inside. Without all the past hurts that come into play, I could simply evaluate each situation, see it and the person involved clearly and make an appropriate response. My inner reaction and my outer response would not be contaminated with all the past hurts, betrayals and invasions I have experienced.

> *Opportunities to separate the trigger from the source present themselves in our daily life all the time. A small thing can set us off into our whole inner world of mistrust. But if we can bring more awareness to these moments, we can begin to separate the present from the past and begin to remove the charge from the trigger.*

And as with all of these bubbles, we also have to know our mistrust history. Why do certain situations in our life today cause us to react so strongly? Why do these situations come up so often? The answer lies in our mistrust history. *Our history will repeat itself.* People will provoke us in much the same way that we were betrayed or invaded in the past. By knowing how this happened when we were younger, it sheds much light on what is happening today.

Also, we have to look closely at our anger and see if we are justifying it unconsciously. For instance, when we get rejected or when something does not go our way, we can feel pain in two ways. One way is what we call, *"pain with fight"*. This is pain with an underlay of anger and resistance to accepting what is. The second way is *"pain with surrender"*. This is feeling the rejection, the loss, or the disappointment with acceptance. In the first case, we are feeding our mistrust; in the second, we are healing it.

The key is taking our energy and focus away from the trigger and placing it on the source - and feeling the wound. It means knowing our own story of invasion and betrayal. That's the origin of our emotional child. When we do that, we gradually react less to the people or events in the present.

> *"People who trust themselves trust others.*
> *People who don't trust themselves cannot*
> *trust anyone*
> *Out of self-trust, trust arises."*
> Osho

Exercises:

1. If you could put your feelings of mistrust into words, what would you say? Allow yourself to express all the mistrust voices that are inside, taking time to write them down as you become

aware of them. These are beliefs that you have about other people and about life.

2. How have these beliefs affected the way that you lead your life, particularly your intimate relationships and' also your relationships with people in general?

3. What kinds of experiences in the past have contributed to your having these mistrust beliefs? How has your experience with invasion and betrayal led to these beliefs?

4. Look over the list of mistrust behaviors and see which ones apply to you. How is this behavior helping you to avoid facing your deep underlying wound of mistrust?

5. In what ways in your present life does your mistrust get triggered? Look at the specific things which people in your life do that bring up your mistrust.

6. Take three of the people closest to you in your life. Look at them through the eyes of your mistrustful wounded child. Write down what you see. Now close your eyes and imagine that you are looking at each one through the eyes of wisdom. Write down what you see. Is there a difference? Does it change when you look at them just as they are without expectations?

Part 4:
BREAKING FREE

Chapter 18:

BREAKING OUT OF OLD PATTERNS

Michael, in one of our seminars, shared that he had just broken up with his girlfriend but he also was still recovering from being abandoned by his wife of 13 years. We asked him why he thought this was happening to him. He said that he realized that he was dependent on women and behaved like a beggar. He thought that eventually, the women who came close to him just got fed up with playing his mother.

"I understand my pattern and I have felt the pain of my abandonment from my mother, but it still doesn't change," he said. When we explored more deeply, it became clear that Michael was deeply identified with his role as a child whenever he came close to a woman. It was true that he was keenly aware of his pattern and had also explored and felt the pain of his early primal wounds. But the pattern persisted because of his identification.

Michael was in his child state of mind when he related to women. He was in a bubble in which he saw himself as a helpless child desperately needing a mother. It is what we call, "abandonment goes shopping." He was aware of it but he was not ready to come out of it because he didn't want to grow up yet. It just wasn't the right time. There was nothing to do but accept the "isness" of the situation.

> *Whenever we are willing to face the fears of being alone, we come out of the identification of our abandoned/ deprived child.*

In my own process, I have seen how my identification with a wounded self-image created my own suffering. As a child, because I always compared myself to my older brother, I formed a self-image of myself as inferior and as a failure. This self-image had haunted me all of my life. I felt it most strongly with my work and creativity where I have had to overcome terrible insecurity. I also have felt it in my relationships with strong men where I re-enacted my trauma with my brother. Eventually, I began to see that this shamed younger brother is just not who I am. It was only a role that I had identified with because so much in my childhood supported it. My shame can still be triggered and I can still enter into the patterns that come from it, but it no longer runs my life. Something has changed inside of me. This change happened gradually and I couldn't say precisely how or why.

Blindly Following a Script
It is our identification with the emotional child that drives our repetitive patterns. To break out of these patterns, our first step is to recognize this identification. It is as though we are a character in a play that is simply following the script that he or she has been given. As long as we are not aware of the script (the identification) the play always remains the same. When we have been traumatized, it creates an identity inside as someone who is defective.

A child always believes that he or she deserves whatever happens to him. When he is abused or humiliated, he believes that it is happening because he is a bad person. This identity sets up an expectation that the trauma will be repeated. It is a *negative expectation*. It also creates the belief in our mind that life is just like that. There are our *negative beliefs*. And finally, it creates deeply ingrained behaviors such as withdrawal, fighting, defensiveness, pleasing and addictions that the child mind has developed to deal with the trauma. These are our *automatic negative behaviors*.

A woman was sharing with us that her relationships with men had always involved her feeling abused sexually.

"I feel that men take advantage of me and make love the way they want without feeling what I want. "

"What happens to you when they are doing that?" We asked.

"I always go along with it and often I end up feeling disgusted. And then I leave the relationship."

We can see how these *negative beliefs, expectations and behaviors* drive the patterns that we may find ourselves in. In her case, it was that she has to satisfy men sexually, that she is not allowed to trust her own way or to express it. Our negative beliefs, expectations, and behaviors take many forms.

a. We *believe* that no one is there for us, that we will never get the love we need and want, and that we cannot trust anyone. We *expect* that people will never give us the love we need and we isolate ourselves and feel deprived of love.

b. We *feel* at a deep place that we are not loveable. We also *expect* that we will be rejected and shamed again. We are waiting for it to happen because at a deep unconscious level, it is all we know. We *attract* people who are not available.

c. We *believe* that we can never be safe if we open; we *expect* that people will abuse or disrespect us and we *attract* situations in which we experience precisely that.

d. We *believe* that other people are selfish; we *expect* that other people will take advantage of us and then we attract people who do that.

Much of our patterns are dictated by *our concept of love*. Our concept of love is based on the role models of our early childhood. It is based on what we observed happening between our parents and it is based on how we were seen and treated. In later life, our attractions are based on this concept of love. If it included abuse, that is what we are attracted to. If it was deprivation, that is what we will be attracted to. Finally, because of our traumas, we have cultivated many behaviors that make it hard for another person to come close to us. For good reason, we have built a wall around ourselves each in our own unique way and it is difficult for others to penetrate this wall or for us to break it down. When we are strongly identified with this abandoned, shamed child, we move into these behaviors instinctively because to this child, it is a question of survival.

Why We Repeat Old Patterns

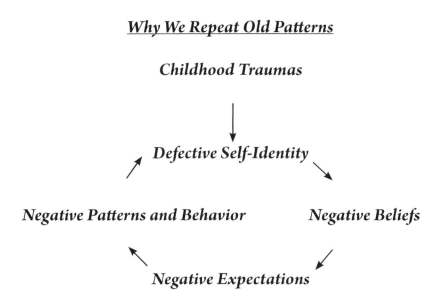

For example, Per, our Norwegian isolated mountain man from a former chapter, is strongly identified with an emotional child who must push people away to feel himself and to feel safe. When someone comes close, he is overwhelmed with an inexplicable primal panic and all he can do is get away. Naturally, he has created a lifestyle of isolation. He feels engulfed and deeply mistrustful. He has no idea that life can be any different because he does not recognize the identification.

When he explored his childhood story, he learned that he was continually invaded and repressed by his controlling, strictly religious mother. He is suspicious that another person only wants to control and manipulate him. He compensates with a pattern of never letting anyone get too close one way or another. He finds himself attracted to people who are "needy", who can be jealous, possessive, emotionally controlling, hysterical and disrespectful of his needs for privacy and aloneness. Naturally, he blames the other person and focuses on what he or she is doing rather than on his own identification.

When we are strongly identified with a child who has been shamed and abused, we hardly know what we want or need. We may settle for any kind of attention, particularly negative attention as an expression of love because it is all we know. Our shock has frozen us in collapse, confusion and inability to feel ourselves. To make the picture even more complex, at a deeper level, part of our identification with a shamed and shocked emotional child is a hunger for revenge. This traumatized child inside has become so mistrustful and has stored so much unconscious unexpressed anger inside that he or she yearns for a time when he feels strong enough to take revenge. In fact, this pressure is so compelling that we often attract someone who can allow us to act out all of these stored resentments.

Maria is a stunning woman. With men, sexuality is more combat than lovemaking. She loves the intensity, she attracts men who are "powerful" and can penetrate her in an aggressive way. She also likes to dominate men with her sexuality. But invariably, her relationships end after several months because she says that "after a while, I don't like the sex anymore." On a deeper level, she has come to see that "a part of me is not there when I make love." That part is her vulnerability that suffered from being sexually desired by her father and physically abused by her mother. Acting out from the wound rather than protecting her wound child while making love keeps her tied to the identification with the wound. The emotional child can see no difference between now and past so it does not matter that we take revenge on a partner or someone working for us now instead of the parent or other person who abused us originally. But in that unconsciousness, there is no healing.

Christina and Alberto, the couple I mentioned earlier who are continually in one drama or another, are both deeply identified with their mistrustful emotional child. Neither of them recognizes how strong is their thirst for revenge. As soon as one of them does something that triggers the other's mistrust, he or she reacts with anger and hurt and is once again convinced that it is better to stay closed and protected. There is really no one there with any wisdom about the intricacies and challenges of relating intimately. Both are totally taken over by their mistrust and the beliefs, expectations and behavior that come from it. It is only natural that their relating involves constant and repetitive games and strategies.

The big question, one that comes up in nearly every one of our workshops, is how to come out of these old patterns? How can we stop repeating the same painful patterns over and over again?

It has four aspects:

How We Break Out of Old Patterns
1. *Recognizing and understanding our identification and the beliefs, expectations, and behaviors that come from it. (Recognition)*
2. *Feeling the pain, shame, and fear that accompany our identification (Immersion).*
3. *Making peace with the pain, shame, and fear of our wounded child whenever it comes up. (Acceptance)*
4. *Taking risks that move us out of the old patterns. (Risk).*

The Four Steps
The first step is the *recognizing stage*. This involves recognizing that we have a pattern, identifying very specifically the negative beliefs, expectations and behaviors that go with it and connecting the pattern to the wound in our emotional child. We trace back from the pattern to the childhood experiences that may have set the process in motion.

For example, imagine that you have a pattern of feeling emotionally abused in your love relationships. You see that you carry the negative expectation that it will always happen. You may even believe that being mistreated is something that is just part of being with someone. You notice what the negative belief and expectations are in your mind when this happens, and you notice how you behave by shrinking in shock and become a compulsive pleaser. Going deeper, you notice that when you think of yourself, you see someone who deserves to be mistreated or rejected. Finally, going back to your childhood, you are aware that your mother or father mistreated you in much the same way that you feel mistreated today.

The second step is more difficult. This is the *immersion stage*. Here, we have to allow ourselves to dive into the experience, feeling it totally. We also need to let go of trying to change it or expecting it to go away. Most of us are naturally impatient to be out of the pattern. But expecting it to change does not resolve it. It is a distraction. Instead, we need to be with it, feeling the fear and pain that it provokes. This phase is not easy to do alone.

I found that I needed some guidance to enter into the experience because my habit of figuring things out and jumping over the fear and pain was so automatic. At a certain point on the journey, having identified the patterns and allowed ourselves to feel them, we have awareness of the negative beliefs, expectations and behaviors. But that is still not enough.

We also need to find a space where we are no longer fighting with the fears, shame or pain that arises. This is step three. A huge aspect of disidentifying from old patterns is finding the space to *accept and embrace* our wounded part inside.

> *We cannot dis-identify from our wounds and from our patterns until we have totally accepted them and allow the feelings whenever they re-occur without resistance or wishing them to go away. As*

> *the resistance goes, then we can choose to stop repeating the patterns. Up until then, they are still running us.*

The final step is to actually *risk* stepping out of pattern and face the fears that come up. For instance, Cynthia, a friend who is in a relationship with a man who tyrannizes her regularly, believes that if she stands up for herself and sets limits, something terrible is going to happen. When she takes risks to do precisely that, she discovers what she was afraid of does not happen. And even when Alex, her boyfriend, gets mad at her, she is fine. Per from Norway believes that if he comes close to someone, he will be taken over. By risking doing it anyway, he slowly discovers that he can stay with himself.

When we are able to risk to do something new and different, it is the beginning of seeing that what we believed about ourselves is not who we are. Michael, in the example I gave in the beginning of the chapter, believes that he is an abandoned child looking for a mother. Whenever he comes close to a woman, that is who is coming to the woman. When we are identifying with being a shamed/abandoned person who is not loveable, that is who is entering into the relationship. The response we get from existence is then predictable.

When we start to dis-identify from the negative self-image, there is a different person in action. We suddenly discover that we are making more intelligent choices and what we always wanted is coming to us. I came out of a pattern of creating relationships where I was a rescuer. Without knowing it, I was following the stages that I have outlined here and the pattern disappeared.

> *"In the world of habits,*
> *It is all repetition.*
> *In the world of consciousness,*
> *There is no repetition."*
> Osho

Exercises:
1. Bringing Awareness to The Pattern.

What are your predominant patterns in your most significant relationships? In bringing awareness to your pattern, notice:

    a. Your negative expectations
    b. Your negative beliefs
    c. You automatic behaviors

E.g. "I have a pattern of being attracted to people who are not available. I find myself always begging for more attention. The other person starts by being available but after some time, finds other priorities in his or her life to be more important. I expect that he or she will give me more time and attention but deep-inside, I expect to be rejected, and when I don't get what I expect, I go into resignation and feel that I will never get the love that I need."

2. Connecting the Pattern to the Wound

    a. How was this pattern similar to events and circumstances in previous relationships and in your childhood? What specifically did you experience as, a child that is similar to what you are experiencing now?

    b. What self-image did you form as a result of these experiences? E.g. "I am a person who is a loser."

Or, "I am someone that does not deserve love."
Or, "I am not attractive."

3. Exploring the Pattern

a.) What are the feelings that this pattern provokes inside? Anger? Hopelessness? Helplessness? Sadness? Panic?

b.) What words would you use to describe the wound? Imagine that your inner child were speaking, e.g. "I feel totally unwanted and unworthy when my partner ignores me when I am talking to him /her." Or "I feel manipulated and controlled when my partner makes demands on me. And it scares me."

4. Taking Risks

What kind of risks could you take in this situation that would challenge the beliefs that your wounded child holds?

5. Dis-identifying from the Pattern

Imagine that you are looking at a small child sitting in front of you. As you look at this small child, become aware that he or she has the same childhood story as you do. He (or she) is as deeply fearful, mistrustful and insecure as you are. Allow yourself to feel this child. You have this child inside of you and yet you have distance from her or him. You can watch when the fears, insecurities and mistrust take over and just allow them to be there but knowing that this is your wounded child which has taken over your consciousness.

Chapter 19:

DEALING WITH PAINFUL EMOTIONS

One of the most challenging aspects of healing our emotional child concerns dealing with painful emotional states when they arise. It is one thing to know our story of how we were shamed and traumatized, but it is quite another to stay present when we get triggered. It is much more challenging to find a way to stay with the experience of intense shame, fear, pain, or shock when these feelings come up in our daily life.

We Were Not Taught How to Be With Painful Emotions
Many of us were raised in an environment where people did not have a healthy way to deal with their emotions. All too often, those who raised us ran away from their fear and pain into some sort of addictive behavior such as substance, sex, or food abuse, working compulsively, becoming aggressive or hysterical, distracting themselves, defending themselves in one way or another, or holding to rigid religious beliefs and morality. Today, we may find ourselves with a tendency to mimic these dysfunctional patterns or pick lovers and friends who do.

Basically, the healing is *to get in touch with the pain and fear that we carry inside*. That is what lies behind our painful emotional states. That may sound simplistic, but it's true. And by "getting in touch", we mean *feeling it and seeing how it shows itself in our body, in our behavior, and in our thinking*. Part of this exploration is also to see how we habitually run away from it – *our compensations*. When we are not choosing to feel our pain and fear, we will find some way of running away from it.

We have explored in the first section all the ways that we act out when we get disturbed. It is human to react in these ways. After all, fear and pain is disturbing and who wants to be disturbed. So, we compulsively try to push away the fear or pain in some way. But instead of stopping there, as most of us might do, we can go further. We can say to ourselves, "Okay, I am disturbed, let me just *feel and be with* this."

A few tools can help:

1. "I am just going to *take a few deep breaths* to give myself some space."
2. "Now, let me take a moment to feel how this *feels in my body* – perhaps I have contraction in my chest or solar plexus, perhaps my breathing is shallow, maybe I feel restless, confused or paralyzed."
3. "If I notice that I am angry, *instead of compulsively acting out* from the anger, let me see how this anger actually feels in my body." "Let me feel the agitation, the tightness, the restlessness, and my desire to strike out." It helped me immensely when I started to look for these body sensations.
4. Alternately, we can notice how *we normally react and behave* when we are disturbed and say to ourselves, "Ok, I am reacting this way because I am disturbed." "Instead of judging myself for being

disturbed and for reacting, I am going to observe this behavior in a nonjudgmental way."
5. "I am also going to notice how the disturbance affects how *I think*." For example, I have judged myself horribly for reacting and even for getting disturbed. My inner dialogue goes something like this, "You idiot, after all these years of working on yourself, and you still go into this stuff!" "You call yourself a meditator! What kind of meditation is this?" "You are impossible! How can you expect anyone to love you?" "Get it together, after all, you teach this stuff, remember?"

When we have a point of view about what we should and should not be experiencing, it makes it very difficult to just be present to it. So it helps to become aware of what our attitude is.

It is hard to accept and explore something that we judge and reject. When we are able to see our self-judgments and opinions, we can stand back from them a bit. We can even question if they are really true.

Noticing How We Get Triggered
No matter how much we may have worked on ourselves or no matter how much time we have spent sitting on a meditation cushion, we are going to get disturbed in certain situations. Life has a way of bringing up whatever is still unsettled inside of us, whatever is still unhealed. And the more we open to life and to love, the more it surfaces – deep spaces of feeling unsafe, unloved or insecure.

Seeing What Wound is Being Triggered
The traumas we experienced as a child had and still have a profound affect on our nervous system. It caused us to lose a basic trust in life and in love. It causes us to be reactive, defensive, withdrawn and irritable. It causes us to experience fear and even profound panic for seemingly no reason. Do we need to know the whole story of how we were traumatized as a child? No. But it is helpful to appreciate that a wound is being triggered and our acting out comes as a result of what we experienced long ago. Without this understanding, we easily judge ourselves.

When fear or pain comes up, it is helpful to know the wound that is being triggered. We call this, *framing*, in our work. Here's an example. When we allow ourselves to get closer to someone, we get more and more attached, and then very small triggers can activate us. And the reason is often the *abandonment wound*. If we are triggered because of a failure or a rejection or if we are anxious because of something that we have to do that is a risk, it is most likely because *our shame wound* is provoked. If we are triggered because someone has done something that we feel is disrespectful, it is likely our mistrust wound has been provoked. Very likely more than one wound that is triggered but for the sake of simplicity, it is good to isolate them.

Learning To Contain and Feel
To use the method we are describing requires a willingness to *contain* uncomfortable feelings. And that's a conscious choice, a conscious commitment, and a clear insight that it is *better to feel than to act out from the feeling*. Acting out is what most of us do until we make this conscious choice. For sure,

that's what I did. But somewhere along the way, I could see that being reactive without going deeper, in the way I have described, was destructive. It was hurtful to those close to me and it re-enforced a childish self-image. Now when I act out, most of the time, I can feel the pain that it causes to others and myself.

I also discovered that I have the space inside to contain the feelings even when in the moment, it feels like I could die. We call that "allowing the burning." Because often that's just how it feels – like burning up inside with anger, frustration, impatience, pain and anxiety. Here's something a bit esoteric that can help us contain those painful or frightening moments. We can open our palms and imagine that we are giving the pain or the fear up to existence (or to God).

Rather than fighting with it, by opening the palms, we surrender to it. This is powerful and it helps immensely for the difficult experience to pass. But *it will pass* and when it passes, it leaves us feeling immensely empowered. It is nourishing to discover that we can hold pain and fear without throwing it on another or distracting ourselves with some addiction. It is also nourishing to notice that when we stop sabotaging our life in reaction, we invite our love and creativity to flourish. People respond to us differently because we are no longer pushing them away with our reactions. Or if we do react, we can apologize and heal the hurt we may have caused by reacting.

> *If you witness anything – fear, anger, hate,*
> *They will disappear,*
> *Leaving a tremendous amount of energy*
> *behind.*

*But if you witness your love, compassion,
kindness, humility,
They will not disappear.
If by witnessing, something disappears, it
was wrong.
And that which is good will become bigger
and bigger.*
Osho

Exercises:
Dealing with Painful Emotional States

Whenever you notice you are disturbed, you can follow these steps:

1. Take a few deep breaths, sit silently or take a walk in nature.
2. Then notice how the disturbance feels in the body.
3. Notice what has triggered your disturbance.
4. Notice, without comment, any thoughts that accompany the disturbance.
5. Notice, again without judgment, if you react and how you react.
6. Decide that you will not resist the experience in any way and give any discomfort up to existence

Chapter 20:

STANDING UP FOR OURSELVES

Most people have a hard time saying "no". Only rarely do we meet people who don't have this difficulty. If we numb ourselves to the fears of our emotional child, we may not have a problem to say no and set limits. But if we are at all in touch with our shame and shock, the slightest confrontation can bring up deep panic.

I have worked with this for years and it is still not easy for me. I hate to say or do anything that might make someone angry with me, cut me off or disapprove of me. It is always a risk for me. I have come to accept that it is just how I am - or rather how my emotional child is. I (my emotional child) hate it when people don't like me. It freaks me out. I think that the world is coming to an end and I feel guilty if I make someone unhappy. But I have learned that I feel much worse when I don't assert my own needs or feelings and compromise. And when I am clear and direct, it always seems to turn out fine.

The Invasion List
Moving out of living a life of compromise is an important step. I have found that in the past, my own compromises were quite automatic and unconscious. Learning about boundaries and starting a process of getting to know and validate my own needs has been deeply empowering for me. Some years ago, Michael, one of my closest friends, was participating in a

men's sharing group in Marin County. He handed me a list that had been given to him by the facilitator of the group on different ways that we invade each other. As I looked down the list, I was amazed at how little I realized about invasion. I was surprised at how many of these "invasive" behaviors I did unknowingly to others. It also validated ways that others had annoyed me but I wasn't clear why. Reading this list, I could understand what was making me angry and withdrawn from these people. Amana and I have used this list as a basis of forming our own list, something we call, *"The Invasion List."*

We ask people, as they go down the list, to consider if this invasion happened to them as a child and if it continues to happen in their lives today. It is natural for people when they go over the list to also notice how they invade others but we do not focus on that. It provokes guilt and guilt is not a good place from which to grow. On the other hand we have found that when we become acutely aware of how invasion happened and happens to us, this awareness brings much deeper sensitivity into our life and then we are less inclined to invade or be invaded.

The Invasion List

1. *Being told what you feel, want, think, or should do.*
2. *Being "set up" - someone breaks a promise, shows up late, does not do what he or she says he would do.*
3. *Having your feelings invalidated, e.g. "You don't need to feel that." "Why are you afraid, there is nothing to be afraid about."*
4. *Being teased. (Unless there is love and trust between two people, teasing can often be abusive.)*

5. *Being patronized, treated as a child, or talked down to.*
6. *Being ignored, not listened to, or cut off. (No one is required to give us attention unless they agree to, but if they do, then we can expect them to be present.)*
7. *Not having your physical space respected, e.g. someone takes something without asking or borrows without returning.*
8. *Someone needs to be right or have the last word.*
9. *Not respecting your "no".*
10. *Being abused with violence or threats (to leave, punish, or hurt you. This violence can come in any form - verbal, energetic, or physical.*
11. *Being demanded upon.*
12. *Being manipulated with anger, guilt, expectations, moodiness, helplessness, illness or sex.*
13. *Inappropriate sexuality (adult to child) or being made love to insensitively.*
14. *Being pressured, criticized, judged, or belittled.*
15. *Being given unsolicited advice.*

Reading and working with this list helped make me more aware how deeply traumatized I actually was and how I continued to allow myself to be invaded or invaded others in much the same way that I was as a child. It was actually quite alarming because suddenly I could understand so much about what children go through. I could see how small aspects of our upbringing that we consider trivial, actually are deeply invasive and shocking.

For instance, my father believed that it was the duty of a parent to encourage children to learn a musical instrument. His intentions were beautiful. He wanted to impart to his children his passion for classical music. But the way he went about it, the standard way Jewish parents instill this teaching, was to force me to study an instrument of his choice - the cello. I never wanted to learn the cello. I would have preferred the guitar but he felt that the classical literature for the guitar was not big enough. He did not believe that I was capable of making this kind of decision on my own. If left to myself, he believed, I would end up only listening to The Beatles and never learn to appreciate Bach or Mozart. I used to joke about how terrible I was at playing the cello but I never realized that this was an invasion. I also never understood why I went into so much shock whenever I was with my teacher. (But as a side note, I am passionate about Mozart's music so the positive aspect of my father's influence worked.)

Setting A Limit Can Provoke Profound Fear
It is common that we have great difficulty becoming aware and affirming our boundaries with those who have some kind of power over us or those whom we look up to. The most obvious is a parent, an employer or a teacher but it is also strong with our lover and friends. My own experience in these situations has been (and still is to some extent) that in these situations, I went into deep shock and had no ability to appreciate or set a limit. I froze; I got confused, and couldn't feel myself.

When we explore what lies underneath this reaction, we can have some compassion for ourselves. Even when I tried to be different, not much changed. In the inner world of my emotional child, when I had given another the power of love or approval over me, I entered into a kind of helplessness. The panic that my child was feeling inside was so great that all I could do was watch it and bring love to this panic. Trying to be different only produced stress, inauthenticity, and withdrawal. On a deeper level, I was also aware that my emotional child needed the world to be loving, sweet, caring, and respectful. I needed the world to be harmonious because otherwise I would feel too threatened.

Overcoming our shock and collapse by becoming comfortable with setting limits is so important a lesson to learn that we will keep creating situations that provoke it. I have seen this both in my own experience and with countless people we have worked with. We are compelled to repeat these situations until we take the risk to stand up for ourselves.

A friend of ours is with a man who often blamed and yelled at her. Her father did the same to her. When this happened, her pattern was to feel guilty and responsible and to excuse herself. She even spiritualized it and said that these moments were helping her to understand more about herself and learn to be less reactive. But her guilt and spiritual excuses only kept her tethered to her self-identity as a victim. Her challenge has been to find the courage to set a limit when someone, her boyfriend or anyone else, yells at her. And, she has done it.

Slowly, she found the courage to express herself when she felt disrespected or blamed. At first, it was hard but with time, it got easier and easier even to the point when she enjoyed the challenge and the energy and self-respect she felt when she did it. It helped her to break the identification with a victimized emotional child that had been with her since childhood. And surprisingly enough, her boyfriend becomes much more respectful because her process mirrored his own which was to learn to stop blaming and accusing. (It is very common that when we enter into our own growth process totally, our intimate partner follows in his or her own way.)

I have another friend who is with a man who flirts compulsively with other women when they are together. She has dealt with this by either complaining to him or feeling sad. Energetically, neither of these two options moves her out of her identification with her victimized emotional child. She does not believe that a man could love her enough to feel satisfied with her. Her challenge is to find the place of dignity inside where his behavior is no longer acceptable to her because it compromises her integrity.

Choosing Dignity Over "Love"
Our emotional child craves for love no matter how meager it is. But as an adult, we cannot live without our dignity. To break our identification with the child, we have to learn to choose dignity over crumbs of love even if it means we have to be alone.

Not all of us respond with shock when we feel invaded. Some of us are more the rage type. But in my experience, the fears underneath are much the same. Also, as I learned more about what my limits were, validated and found the courage to affirm them, I moved from shock to rage. In the past, the lag time between the invasion and the recognition of an invasion was quite long - days, even weeks. I would notice that for some reason, I was not feeling very good about the person.

Or, I would notice that I began to judge them and might even judge them with others. That became a good indication for me that I had compromised, not said something I needed to say, and was feeling resentful.

But gradually the lag time shortened and as it did, my fire also came more quickly. My increased awareness of how I was compromising myself and had done so in the past seemed to kindle the flame of the rage that I had repressed. This was a good phase for me but I saw eventually that just being able to feel the invasion and react with anger was not the end of the process by any means. My anger was still coming from my emotional child who was carrying a lifetime of resentment. Reacting with rage is not setting limits. There is no real power in reaction. It is still just the emotional child having moved from collapse to explosion. Yes, explosion is better in many ways that collapse, resentment, and passive aggression, because it has energy but it is still immature.

I had to ask myself, what was I angry about? And what was the purpose of the anger? Part of the anger was the belief that if I didn't react immediately, I would not be safe. People will only take advantage of me if I don't fight back. Another part of it was coming from my expecting the person or situation to be different. I could not go of the hope that the world will always be loving, caring, and considerate. These magical beliefs were causing me to wear blinders. Either I minimized, denied, or ignored it when I felt invaded by someone or I would get righteously indignant.

In the first case, I would say to myself, "He or she just was thinking of other things." "I don't really care, it's no big deal." "He always does that kind of thing." "I need to learn to be more tolerant." "I don't need to be so uptight." And then I would support these statements with all kinds of spiritual beliefs. "Good people are tolerant and flexible." "I am a better person when I don't make a big deal about this." These attitudes actually invited people to invade me because I was sending out a vibration, which said, "You can do whatever you like with me, I won't mind."

At a certain point, I would go to the other extreme. Outrage. "How could you do that to me?" "How can you be so insensitive and selfish?" "I don't do that to you!" And then I would want nothing to do with that person or take revenge in all kinds of creative ways. This duality between denial and rage underlies our experience of invasion. Until I understood that it was being fed by unconscious expectations, I could see I was dooming myself to perpetually go back and forth between hope and disappointment, collapse and rage.

> *The emotional child clings to the hope that people will be how we want them to be and therefore alternates between collapse and explosion. We need to recognize that the emotional child will always be in this duality. But our ability to set limits ultimately comes from beginning to see people and situations as they are and responding appropriately by dealing with each situation in a centered way.*

Reaction Or Response?

Some years ago, I was involved a bit in a controversy with a colleague of mine. He wrote me a venomous letter that included personal attacks that were not relevant to the issue we were disagreeing about. It was clearly an insensitive invasion. When I received the letter, I could feel the rage that his attack provoked. In the past, my way would have been to try and create harmony or attack back in the same vein. Instead, I sat with the feelings for three days and then responded, clearly setting my limits but also admitting how I might have invaded him.

I cite this example because in my own experience with this issue of setting limits, there comes a time when we gradually have less of a need to throw our reaction on the other person. We may still feel it inside but we are able to let the feelings be there. We can allow time for clarity to surface and respond accordingly.

Ultimately, I can see that my learning to set boundaries has nothing whatsoever to do with the other person. It comes from clarity. This is a clarity about what I need for myself and a clarity to see people as they are rather than how I wish them to be. I begin to understand that everyone has unconsciousness and that unconsciousness leads to insensitivity, invasion, disrespect, and even abuse. As this understanding deepens, I slowly stop setting myself up to be hurt, abused, or disappointed because I see things clearly. Also, when I am not so addicted to getting crumbs of attention and approval, I am much more able to say "no" to what does not feel right inside. I develop an inner sense for when something just feels right and when it doesn't.

But making this shift means we have to constantly face our fears of abandonment, rejection, punishment, or disapproval. When we find ourselves continually feeling hurt by someone, we are just not seeing that person as she or he is. Holding him or her up in our ideals and expectations prevents us from feeling the frightening aloneness that comes when we wake up out of our dream. If we start to say "no", the person might think we are selfish. Or worse, he or she might take revenge. It is safer and more familiar to compromise. This is how our emotional child thinks and operates.

> *But with awareness about invasion, we develop choice. We can recognize when an invasion happens, feel the fear, and eventually set a limit anyway, sometimes even without any reaction. But it is not a linear process. With some people and in some situations, we find that we have clarity. And, with others, our shock or rage can easily be provoked.*

The Stages of Learning to Set Limits

Stage 1: Feeling and accepting shock and being aware of invasion.

Stage 2: Feeling the rage and observing our reaction.

Stage 3: Clarity – setting a limit with necessary, responding with centeredness, seeing people as they are; willing to be with our aloneness; being connected to our own needs and priorities.

> *Live in Insecurity!*
> *Live in revolution!*
> *Be a rebel, risk,*
> *Because nothing is ever attained in life*
> *Without risk.*
> *The more you risk,*
> *The closer you are to God.*
> *When you risk all, all is yours.*
> *Osho*

Exercises: The Process of Setting Limits
1. Stage One: Validating Shock
    a) Look over the invasion list and ask yourself:
- Is this happening in my life today and if so with whom?
- Did this same item, occur for me in the past and if so, with whom?
- Which of these items affect me the most?
- Do I do this to others in my life today?

    b) When you feel invaded, how does it feel inside? Write down what you observe.

2. Stage Two: Feeling the Rage and Watching Your Reactions
    a) When you notice that you have felt invaded by someone, take the time just to feel the rage that it provokes. How does it feel inside? Where do you feel it?

    b) If you move into reaction, watch your reactions and let them be there.

    c) When you feel invaded by someone, what is your belief of what would happen if you don't do something?

3. Stage Three: Clarity
    a) When you feel invaded, stop and ask yourself, "What am I expecting from this person?" Then answer the question, "I am not willing to let go of this expectation because..."

b) Imagine that you had glasses of clarity. If you put on those glasses with someone with whom you feel invaded or betrayed, what do you see?
c) Notice the difference of how it feels inside when you are compromising and when something feels right to you.
d) Notice if there is something that you would need to say that would bring more dignity to yourself.

Chapter 21:

REPRESSION, EXPRESSION, AND CONTAINMENT

I once read a book about the famous samurai warrior, *Musashi* by Eiji Yoshikawa. It was one of the most extraordinary books I have ever read. It tells the story of how Musashi became the most renowned of all samurai in Japan's history. The whole book, over 1000 pages long, relates how he learned to develop a deeper and deeper degree of centeredness.

In this journey, he sets aside his anger, to accept sadness and grief as part of life and to keep his focus unfettered and undistracted by emotion, greed, or ambition. This man's power came not so much from his skills as a fighter but from his inner development. It came from his ability to contain energy. In the beginning of the story, he is a wild and undisciplined man. He is living totally in his emotional child state. His teacher locks him in a room for two years to quiet his restless nature (the Japanese approach) and then leads him through one life test after the next. Many of them involve no fighting at all. Musashi's story has always inspired me. It shows so beautifully how we drain our life force and our power in all the ways that we leak our energy.

> *There is a big difference between feelings and emotions. Feelings are energy experiences that arise from moment*

> *to moment and have no prior history. Emotions are experiences that are strongly affected by feelings that were not felt in the past and therefore are contaminated by the past and also by our opinions about the feeling.*

One of our principle energy leaks comes from how we deal with our feelings and energy – grief, anger, sexuality and joy. We leak our energy when we repress our feelings and we often leak it when we express them as well. We stop leaking when we learn to contain them. Containment is just being present to them – nothing more. The emotional child has no ability to contain anything – it either represses or expresses automatically and unconsciously.

Containment vs. Repression
Containment comes from learning to watch the emotional child – to watch how it deals with feelings and energy. The difference between containment and repression is that in containment, we are connected to the feeling and flow of energy inside and we can choose whether or not to express it. When the energy is repressed, we don't have that choice. Also, when the expression of feelings and energy is in the hands of our emotional child, we cannot choose either to not express, we just react.

> *To reach a point of containment, we first have to understand what our relationship to feelings has been for us in our life and is now. The answer lies mostly in how we learned to relate to our feelings and energy as a child. This is the first step.*

CHAPTER 21: REPRESSION, EXPRESSION, AND CONTAINMENT

Although unspoken, the basic conditioning I received about emotions was to deny, ignore, judge, avoid, or suppress them. It wasn't until much later that I realized that the reason for such a negative approach to feelings was fear. My parents, and actually most of the adults I encountered as a child, were terrified of their feelings. As a child, I hardly ever saw either of my parents express anger, sadness, fear, or even joy.

When people are afraid of something they naturally control it. Especially something like feelings that so easily take us out of control. Strong feelings such as outbursts of anger or powerful expressions of grief used to make me very uncomfortable. I did not realize it was because I was terrified of them. And, I was terrified of them only because I was not familiar with any outward expression of feeling. The whole world of emotion was cloaked in shadows for me.

We also may have repressed our feelings because it was just too painful and frightening to feel them. Most of us experienced deep pain as a child but to function and to deal with this incredible pain, we learned to bury our feelings and often simply disconnect from them. Furthermore, being alive, spontaneous, sensuous, sexual, powerful, joyful, and outrageous may not have fitted with the moralistic conditioning that many of us were raised in.

We may have been conditioned to be mediocre and to hold down our energy. To be angry or powerful was too threatening for most of the home environments and societies that we were grew up in. Few of us were lovingly supported to feel and express our losses and disappointments either. Too often it is covered with denial and we probably received the message that it is a sign of weakness or collapse to feel fear or pain.

Repressed Emotions Can Lead to Hysterics or Control
Some people's history with expressing feelings may have been quite different from mine. In their childhood environment, feelings may have been expressed in an extreme way. This kind of conditioning can be deceptive because it may seem that this kind of environment is a healthy approach to feelings. On the contrary, it is not really "feeling" but avoidance of feeling – a kind of hystericism driven by fear.

It can be quite alarming to realize that even when someone is exploding in rage or shedding copious tears, they are actually not present and not experiencing the feelings at all. Basically, most of us have learned to feel and express our feelings and energy in distorted, perverted, or addictive ways. They come out in ambitious, greedy, political, aggressive, and insatiable ways. When our natural feelings and energy are not supported, two things happen. The first is that they simply get buried and we collapse. The second is that they come out in an excessive and distorted way.

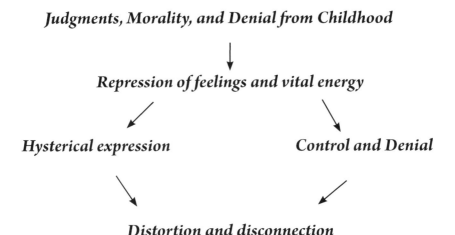

CHAPTER 21: REPRESSION, EXPRESSION, AND CONTAINMENT

Years ago, before I explored my own world of feelings, I was following a very intensive path as a yogi. I was living in an ashram, doing yoga and meditation four hours a day starting very early in the morning and going to medical school in between. I even dressed in all white clothes and, much to the horror of my parents, wore a white turban on my head. This lasted about three years. After I had graduated from medical school and moved to California to do a residency in family medicine, I was still wearing white clothes and a turban but I had reduced the yoga practice to about one hour a day. I suspected that something was not complete in my approach to inner growth; especially since my relationship was a disaster and this life of discipline was a bit dry - to say the least. A friend told me of a workshop called, "Lifespring" that worked with feelings.

I booked it. On the first day, standing up in front of the staff and introducing myself, I was told that I was a phony, that I was totally disconnected and that I had no idea who I was. (It was done a bit in the old confrontational style that was popular in the seventies, but I got the point.) A few hours later, we were asked to sit in front of a chair and just say the word, "hate!" over and over again, seeing what came up. This went on for about an hour with all the lights out. As the time went by, things started to happen inside. I ripped off the turban and started to go wild. When the lights came on, I quickly found the turban again and put it on.

But not for long. As the workshop progressed, we came to a point where we were asked to make a statement affirming our nature. When someone felt his sentence and it seemed right, everyone cheered and danced around the room. I kept standing up with statements like, "I am a committed spiritual seeker" or "I am following the path of truth." Each time everyone booed. Finally, the trainer asked me to go home, change my clothes, shave my beard, put on shorts and a tee shirt, and take off the turban or not to bother to return.

At first, I was offended and felt that "my spirituality" was being put down. But at home, I looked in the mirror for the longest time and it hit me that the trainer was totally right. I returned some hours later. The participants were patiently waiting for me because I was the only one who had not completed the process. I got up and gave my essence statement, "I am a playful and vulnerable person." Everyone cheered and carried me around the room on their shoulders. They had a lot of energy for such a tough case as I was.

That was only the beginning of my journey to rediscover my feelings and my energy. Not long after that, I went to India to the ashram that would become my home for many years and embarked on an extended program of workshops and meditation retreats lasting for years. This was a rather unique place that combined Western style therapy with Eastern meditation. During an initial interview shortly after I arrived, the person speaking to me suggested that I spend the first month doing only workshops dealing with the body. "You seem to be quite focused in the mind with lots of ideas about who you are and how you should be. It's all rubbish. I feel that it would be good for you to let go of all this and just to spend time reconnecting with your body." She was absolutely right.

Over the next several months, I worked intensely with mountains of repressed anger and grief that I had stored inside. I explored my repressed sexuality and I learned a new approach to meditation that was not based on holding down my energy. I could see how strongly I had denied, judged, and repressed my feelings and my energy. They were sitting on my vitality and spontaneity like a huge weight pushing them down.

These judgmental voices were sides of my personality that spiritualize and have an agenda for how I should be. They told me that it was better to be "nonreactive" and "together" rather than expressive and demonstrative. Or, "I don't have any anger or sadness inside." "I have already been through all of that." "Anger and sadness are negative emotions that are not good to indulge." "My way of seeking truth no longer requires digging into all that stuff." It took many years to penetrate these repressive forces of judgment and denial but now I realize that it is all rubbish.

Expression Burns Away Old Repressive Habits
Because of all our repression, judgment, and denial, most of us have to go through a period where we uncover the expressiveness of our emotional child. At least, that has been my experience. I needed to allow all that energy to be expressed freely and openly until I once again become intimately reacquainted with all the feeling and aliveness that was shut down so long ago. The expression burned through the repression and it altered my sense and experience of myself from someone who was shut down and afraid of feelings and energy to someone who could feel and express them.

> *For many of us, our experience of feelings and energy is full of shame, contempt, and self-judgment. We believe that we are cowardly or insensitive, that we are collapsed or violent, irresponsible, or*

> *too serious, that we are too sexual or too inhibited. All of these negative self-concepts hold down our feelings and our energy.*

When I brought my energy out of repression, I had to pay close attention to these judgments. I could judge myself for not being enough and then judge myself for being too much. And, whenever I began to express what was repressed, my inner voices were always there to take bites out of my behind when I risked exploring unfamiliar ground. Our judgments come from the ways we were conditioned. Whenever we stray from our conditioning, our judgment and guilt acts up. I judge precisely what I learned to condemn. I judge what I see in myself or others that I was taught were bad. But when we don't allow the feelings or the energy to be there and be expressed, it will come out in many distorted ways. Greed, intense sexual desires, ambition, revenge, control, and manipulative strategies all comes from not having a healthy relation to our feelings and our energy, allowing them to be there and to move as they want to move.

Somewhere along the way, I told myself that I was going to make a commitment to express rather than repress. I was going to give myself the permission and to take the risk to express the wildness and freedom that I had missed. To say what I had held back. To make love when and how I wanted to. To take risks and put myself out in ways that I had not allowed myself to do in the past. To expose instead of hiding. To notice how I hid behind my pleasing, quiet, rescuing and polite roles. To be honest and to risk something new no matter how frightening.

My irritability has always been a good signal to me that I am holding something inside. We get irritable when we are covering a desire - perhaps by being a nice person and doing the "right thing", rescuing someone and denying our own wants. But if we do what we want to do, we risk being judged or rejected. Instead, we repress and get irritable. By noticing when we get irritable and asking what we wanting at that moment, it often uncovers something we are repressing. It is similar with moments when we are complaining or assuming an inferior, obsequious role with someone.

When we are not natural and spontaneous with our life energy, it can show itself in our daily life in all kinds of ways - health problems, difficulties with sex and intimacy, stifled creativity, crippling feelings of inferiority, or frequent mood changes. We can be easily irritable, reactive and defensive, passive aggressive, constantly comparing ourselves to others.

There are many therapeutic devices that attempt to bring us out of repression, but we found that when we start to uncover our fear and shame, our repressed energy and feelings surface on their own. In our experience resurfacing our buried energy and feelings happens best in an atmosphere that is relaxed, allowing, non-pressuring, deeply caring, and extremely patient.

In my own journey, I did many processes that encouraged me to put out my rage in safe environments where I could experience this energy without fear of hurting myself or anyone else. Those experiences were wonderful and extremely helpful. Then I moved deeper and began working with profound inner spaces of fear and shock. I began to connect with how much trauma I had inside and how much it still affected my life today. This was a different kind of work, in some ways more subtle than the catharsis I had done. In fact, I needed to let go of the catharsis in order to reach these places inside.

Each of us has to find our own way of recovering the energy that was repressed and each of us may need different approaches. But we find that it is deeper and more intimate when feeling arise spontaneously; when anger arises from an inner space when we connect with our lost need and right to assert our individuality, dignity, and integrity, when sexuality arises from the heart, and when sadness comes as our heart opens.

Learning Containment

The final step on this journey of recovering feelings is learning containment. At a certain point, I felt that I was sufficiently reconnected to my feelings and energy that my focus naturally shifted. I had learned to express and to be comfortable with expressing. It seemed more challenging to be present to what was inside without feeling compelled to do anything. While I was uncovering repressed energies, I was giving free rein to my emotional child. But the journey became different. It shifted to watching the emotional child.

When this child is in control, uncomfortable feelings like pain, fear, anger and guilt are difficult to hold inside and be with. There is a strong desire to get rid of them in some way. But with more awareness, I seemed to develop more space inside - more self-love, more understanding, more ability to tolerate frustration and disappointment, and more ability to hold discomfort inside. George Gurdjieff, in the opening chapter of his book, *Meetings With Remarkable Men*, tells the story that as his father was dying, his present to him was a small piece of advice. He told him that if anyone made him angry, he should wait twenty-four hours before responding in anyway. His last will and testament to his son was to learn containment.

With containment, it is not that we don't express but the expression is no longer driven by the emotional child. We can choose and our choice is governed by what feels natural and appropriate. The focus is on being with the feelings and energy that arise inside and becoming sensitive to their natural spontaneous flow. It is like coming home to a fullness of our feeling and alive nature when it is freed from judgments and repression.

In the past, I judged myself for not being feeling or energetic enough. But I have noticed that when I am just present to what is there and not concerned with impressing or influencing another, I get to know my own way of feeling and my own energies. It has been and continues to be a beautiful experience to come to trust myself in this way because it brings me a much deeper relaxation and silence inside. I am hidden and solitary in my feelings. They live deep inside of me and are very private.

But when I don't interfere with pressure or judgment, they come out in their own special way and time. One of the principle areas of our work in seminars is to guide people to discover the nature of their own energies and emotions, patiently and spaciously. In this journey of discovery, it doesn't matter if we are connected or disconnected, alive or collapsed, open or closed, we just stay present to what is on the screen. Sometimes it is shock, collapse, numbness, and confusion. Other times, it may be irritation or rage, sadness, or restlessness. We just watch and allow, openly and lovingly, honoring our own unique emotional nature.

From Repression to Expression to Containment

Step 1: The Awareness of Repression
    a. *Watching your judgments of your feelings and energy*
    b. *Watching your irritability.*
    c. *Watching your complaining and collapse.*

Step 2: Moving into Expression
    a. *Having a safe place to express.*
    b. *Making a commitment to risk expressing verbally, sexually, and energetically*
    c. *Allowing the energy to arise without pressure.*

Step 3: Containment
    a. *Learning to be with the feelings and energies inside without judgment or pressure.*
    b. *Feelings and energy no longer in the compulsive control of the emotional child. There is choice whether to express or not.*
    c. *Coming home to our unique emotional nature by watching the natural and spontaneous flow of our emotions and energy.*

> *"It is perfectly good to go deeper into your feelings*
> *But remember one thing,*
> *The one who is going deeper is separate from them*
> *You are the witness, so as you go deeper,*

You will come across many things
Which you have suppressed.
But you are as pure as a mirror."
Osho

Exercises:
1. Bringing Awareness to Repression:
   a. Notice closely the judgments that you have about feeling and expressing sadness or anger. Notice any judgments you have about feeling or expressing sexuality or joy.
   b. What messages were you given about feeling and expressing these?
   c. Notice closely during the day the times that you get irritable. In these moments, ask yourself, "What am I wanting right now?" "What am I doing to hide this desire?"
   d. Notice closely the situations where you feel inferior. What are you feeling at these moments toward the person you feel inferior to?
   e. Notice the times when you are complaining. At these moments, what energies might you be repressing?

2. Expression:
   a. What are your fears if you express anger, sadness, joy or sex? Fear of ridicule? Fear of being too much? Fear of failure? Fear of punishment?
   b. Expression Contract - You may want to make an inner commitment to yourself to take a risk to express in these areas what in the past you might have repressed.

3. Containment:
Begin to watch your feelings and energies as they arise – sex, anger, sadness, guilt, fear, greed, or any kind of desire. Notice:
    a. How each one feels in the body, where you feel it and how it affects your breathing?
    b. What is the natural flow of this feeling or energy free of judgment or pressure?

Chapter 22:

SEX AND THE EMOTIONAL CHILD

When we make love, we get vulnerable. Especially if we start to open to someone in a deeper and more committed relationship. And when we are vulnerable, our emotional child usually takes over our consciousness. Yet we seldom realize how deeply our sexuality is in the hands of our emotional child. There are few situations where our wounds are more exposed than in making love. Unless we have some understanding for how these wounds are being exposed, it is easy for us to move into one of the automatic behaviors of the emotional child when we are making love. Then our sex life can become addictive, reactive, dreamy, or full of compromise and expectation.

If we don't want to feel the vulnerability that comes up when we make love, we have to do something to hide it either from our lover or ourselves. Our fears of being left, of being humiliated, of being engulfed, or of being hurt or abused are so strong that we may use all kinds of compensations to avoid feeling or showing them. This creates problems because we would like to melt deeply with another person but our fears and protections seem to get in the way. In my experience, it is not possible to come close to someone in love unless we have developed some understanding for how our wounds get triggered in sex and the ways that we use to cover them up.

A couple we saw recently came because they were having sexual problems. The man admitted that he was having an affair with another woman.

"This new woman is not demanding sexually. But my wife is driving me crazy with her sexual expectations. She is so demanding that whenever I start making love with her, I lose my erection. With my new partner, I have no trouble staying hard. But to be honest, I don't really want to continue this affair. I am still deeply in love with my wife but I am a total loss for how to deal with the sexual difficulties that we are having."

"It's true," she responded. "I am demanding and I am making a great deal of effort to bring awareness to it. Yet I feel that I am so demanding because he is not available and part of the reason that I am so demanding is because I want to be reassured that he loves me."

How The Emotional Child Shows Up in Lovemaking
When our emotional child carries a deep fear of being abandoned or feels deprived of love and security, it easily comes out in the ways we relate sexually. We can become demanding or we can become withholding. Both behaviors are covers for our terror of being left. We asked the couple if each one of them would be willing to express to the other what they need to feel safe and loved.

He said, "First of all, I need to know that you are accepting me the way I am and letting me have the space I need to do my own thing. I love you and I'm committed to you but I can't stand your constant demands. When I feel all that demanding energy, I just want to go away. And, it's a total turn off for me sexually."

She said, "I hear you and I don't want to shock you with my demands. But I need to know that you really want to be with me and that you are willing to take time for us to be together." He was able to hear her concerns and fears.

His emotional child reacts with distance and acting out with other women when he feels suffocated and demanded upon. But if he can learn to set limits when he wants time and space for himself and is willing to make time to be available to her, he is moving from his emotional child to his mature adult. Her emotional child acts out with demands when she feels that she is not getting the love she wants. If she can learn to contain her fears and realize that it is not his job to fill her emptiness, she is moving from her emotional child to her mature adult.

Shame, Shock, Fear, and Dysfunction in Lovemaking

The intimacy of lovemaking can also bring up our fear, shock, and shame as strongly as any other situation in our life. A person who has been sexually abused in some way will very likely have terrifying fears when he or she comes close to another person sexually. Often we don't even know what is happening but our body remembers and responds to protect us in some way. We may space out or our body just doesn't work. But we don't need to have been sexually abused as a child to experience severe shame and shock in our sexuality.

For instance, if we sensed as a child a strong energy of repression and condemnation around sex, that is enough to create dysfunction for us. Our sexuality can be one of the main symptoms of trauma. Impotence, premature coming, difficulties with orgasm, tightness or pain in our genitals can all be manifestations of our shame and shock. They can come from any form of unconscious sexual or non-sexual trauma. For instance, many men have deep fears of being castrated by overbearing, controlling female energy and women have deep fears of being abused by aggressive, insensitive male energy. There also is the fear of being shamed, of not satisfying the other person and then having them leave us because we are not good lovers.

For many of us, it is much too frightening even to admit these fears to ourselves, let alone share them with our lover. Instead, we compensate. Our strategies for covering our fears in sex can be very creative. And, because sex is such a charged area, we seldom see how we have moved into compensation. One way we compensate is to try to control the other person in any way we can. We demand, expect, teach, cut off, or overpower. We can move into sexual performance. On the other extreme, we may cover our fears by spacing out or collapsing in self-judgment. The fears are too great.

The easiest way out seems to be to let the body continue going through the motions to making love but our consciousness goes elsewhere. It can take only a mille-second for us to go into shock and dissociate. We usually have no idea what has happened.

The slightest trigger can bring back a hidden trauma and we are gone. In the same way, the slightest trigger can also fill us with shame and humiliation and our energy shrinks. All of a sudden, we feel terrible and want only to get away and hide in our shame. Or, to find some way to cover it up by working harder or pushing harder. We can become like a sexual machine going through the motions but underneath and perhaps without even knowing it, we are in shame.

In a recent seminar, a woman shared with us that she only feels attracted to men who are emotionally unavailable and potentially violent. The only way she gets excited is when the sex is hot and on the edge of violent. Sensitive and loving men bore her. She has no memory of sexual trauma from her past and is not interested in changing the way she has sex. Still, she misses deeper intimacy. We suggested that she continue the way she is going if that is what she wants but to be aware of two things. First, to observe how she feels emotionally and how her body reacts during and after sex. Secondly, her choice of men would probably not lead to deeper intimacy because there is no basis of safety. In our understanding, this is making love on the trauma level. When she feels motivated to change this pattern, she would have to get into a deeply committed course of psychotherapy.

When our emotional child grips our sexuality, we traumatize each other. At times, we can be deeply collapsed and other times, we want (and need) to go wild and not have anything or anyone interfere with our sexual energy. The wildness is often just a natural reaction to all the repression we have experienced. But one person's wildness can put another person in shock. Then the one who is feeling wildness feels repressed by the other person's shock and collapse. It is painful on both sides and when two lovers have not built up trust and sensitivity between them, this polarity causes much hurt, misunderstanding, and even separation.

I have experienced a great deal of shame and inner struggle around my sexuality. When I found myself coming closer to someone, I became more sensitive and my insecurities became much more easily provoked. The result would be that I would be premature. I have done just about everything to overcome this. I went to sex therapists, I practiced Taoist and Yogic exercises, squeezed this, tightened that, breathed through one nostril, stood on my head - nothing really worked. At times in the past, I felt so humiliated and hopeless that I felt like giving up sex completely. But with Amana, it ceased to be a problem. The symptoms didn't all disappear but because there is so much love and caring between us what matters is our connecting, not the technique. In that atmosphere, we can allow each other everything. It isn't textbook perfect but I am not competing with anyone anymore.

Dramas in Lovemaking
When our emotional child has control of our sexuality and we are not aware of it, everything can become a problem. One person's emotional child triggers the other's and soon it is no longer two adults attempting to make love but two frightened, mistrusting, shamed children facing each other. Furthermore, in these situations it is impossible to communicate or feel safe enough to reveal anything. We are charged with hurt and betrayal.

But when we become conscious how and why our emotional child gets triggered in sex, everything can change. First of all, we have to be conscious that this is an arena where our betrayal, our anger at being repressed or our deep insecurities and fears may easily get provoked. It is naive, in my experience, to imagine that we can enter into a deepening sexual relationship without all of this coming up. It is precisely one of the reasons we desire intimacy - to heal.

I have a friendship with a couple that I have known for many years. For a long time, their sexuality was a disaster. She felt that he was insensitive; he felt that she was holding down his fire. But they had such love for each other that they resolved to get through it. In the course of working with herself, she discovered a past history of sexual abuse, which explained why she had so many fears related to having sex with a man. He came to understand what happens for someone with this kind of past and it enabled him to approach their lovemaking in a new way.

From his side, he recognized the ways that his wildness had been repressed as a child and how sometimes this energy also carried anger for his being suppressed. He also came to understand that sometimes he was inappropriately acting out his need for wildness in sex and channeled it into other areas - like dancing and doing shamanic rituals. Now their sexuality has transformed. Both took responsibility to work with their own issues and also to see how their emotional child was affecting their beloved. And they have shared with us that when they make love now, they can experience and share whatever comes up - from terror, to tears, to gentle melting, to total wildness.

Levels of Lovemaking
In our workshops, we use a simple drawing to help illustrate the ways that we bring awareness to the role of the emotional child in our sexuality.

On Level 1, the top layer, where we usually live in most of the time, we are lost in unconscious strategies to cover up our fears and insecurities. Here, all the behaviors of the emotional child come out and get acted out on the other. There is no communication because there is no awareness. Each person is primarily concerned with getting his or her needs and wants met and the other person's feelings are not such a priority.

On Level 2, we begin to be present to the fears, insecurities, and shock that may be provoked while making love. We begin to become sensitive to our wounds - our shame and shock, our feelings of betrayal, our mistrust and our fears of being left or rejected. We become aware of how the other person triggers these wounds and how we have automatically reacted in the past.

And, finally, Level 3, the bottom layer, is the space when we can both melt or go wild with each other in an atmosphere of trust, understanding, and intimacy. We have the sensitivity to feel where either one of us is emotionally and energetically. There is a blending and accommodating. I have found, at least in my own experience, that another characteristic of this level is that both people take the focus off orgasm or performance.

When that the focus is on orgasm, it is usually a clear invitation for the emotional child to enter in with expectations and frustrations. On the third layer, the focus is on connection. As with every map that we use in the work, it is not that one level is better than another but rather a help to see and feel where we are at any moment. This awareness alone carries us naturally to deeper levels of consciousness. Without a goal or preference, we can observe ourselves without the normal mountains of self-judgment.

Sex and the Emotional Child
Level 1: The Emotional Child in Strategies
Control, Expectations, Demands, Entitlement, Revenge, Reaction, Addiction
Layer 2: The Emotional Child in Wounds
Shock, Shame, Dysfunction, Guilt, Fears of Abuse, Fears of Being Left or Rejected, Fears of Engulfment or Humiliation
Level 3: Maturity
Melting, Trust, Relaxation, Free Flow of Energy, Connection, Not Focusing on Orgasm, Sex Hot or Soft Depending on the Moment

Accept life as it is
In all its naturalness
And live it in its totality.
The very totality will lift you day to day
Step by step.
If sex is coal, one day the diamond of love
will also manifest from it.
This is the first key.
Osho

Exercises: Bringing Awareness to Your Emotional Child in Sex

1. Begin to observe yourself while making love.
   a. Notice when you feel fear, insecurity, inadequacy, or frustration.
   b. Notice what specifically triggers you to feel these things.
   c. Notice what you do in these situations - how you normally react.
   d. Notice if you blame the other person for these feelings.
2. Now, notice what lies underneath your normal reactions and defenses.
   a. What fears are being provoked?
   b. Carefully review each of the five wounds – shame, shock, mistrust, engulfment, and abandonment and write down how in sex, this wound might be provoked.
3. What is it like for you to express these fears to your partner? Ask yourself "How would it be for me to reveal this or these fears to him or her?"

4. Take some time to explore and perhaps write down what your strongest desires and longings are related to your sexuality with another.

Chapter 23:

BREAKING OUT OF THE PRISON OF ROLES

In my childhood, I got a strong message that the only real profession was medicine. My parents said, both verbally and nonverbally, that it was fine whatever I wanted to do with my life (as long as it was becoming a doctor.) Neither of my parents were doctors. My father was prevented from going to medical school because of insufficient funds and poor eyesight.

My mother practiced medicine from the medicine chest in the bathroom into which she shored the most creative assortment of potions, salves, and pills that she had collected in all the different countries we had lived in. One of her favorites was an Italian skin ointment that she insisted healed everything from skin infections to allergic reactions to mosquito bites. My brother, who also went into medicine, once bought her a copy of Harrison's *Textbook of Medicine* so she could improve her skills. She treated it as bedtime reading.

I was conditioned to adopt the role of a doctor to feel worthy as a person. Don't get me wrong. I still have incredible reverence for the profession of medicine and consider it, if done in the right spirit, as one of the highest of callings. In fact, the sentence in Oath of Hippocrates, "Above all do no harm", that every medical student reads at graduation, guides me all the time in my work with people.

Finding Roles That Reflect Our Essential Nature
But I had to find my own way rather than following blindly the path set out for me. Even though the forces of my conditioning were very strong, I also had an equally strong force inside which wanted me to find myself. After college, I started medical school but dropped out after only a week. For years, I struggled to find my way. I spent two years in the domestic Peace Corps (VISTA), a horrible year in law school, and two years as a hippie living in communes in Oregon and California.

Then I went back to medical school. I knew that I was destined to work with people in some way and when it came to deciding what to do with my life (being a hippie just didn't quite do it for me), all I could think of was medicine. I went through medical school and a residency in Family Medicine before I realized that working with physical illness was "not my thing". I eventually found my home leading workshops and doing individual and couples work that help people to love themselves and others. But it was a long journey to find and trust my own way.

Most of us have been conditioned to fulfill the expectations of others rather than learning and being guided and supported to find our own way. When we are not supported and encouraged to discover our unique individuality, we develop with a basic feeling of shame and doubt about our ability to master life. We do not have a sense of who we are. We are left with a deep hunger to find ourselves and to discover the self-confidence that we never found earlier.

Many people who work with us are living a life and living in a relationship that makes them unhappy and unsatisfied. Oscar created a family of three children with a woman he has been with for 22 years and says that he never loved her but hasn't been able to leave because of too much guilt. Martin has been working in a law firm for thirty years but he hates it. He is too afraid to leave because he does not know how he could support his family. He has always wanted to be a landscaper but felt that that career was not distinguished enough.

It brings amazing happiness to our core when we are doing what we know deep inside, we are meant to do. It is as if we have found the way in which the divine energy of existence wishes to manifest itself through us. This is a realization that comes from inside and is not of the mind. When we listen to our mind, it is usually rational, fear-based, and coming from messages we received and may continue to receive from family. Often to find our unique manifestation, we have to distance ourselves from these messages and also from our fear and trust our guts.

Our Identification With Roles Becomes A Prison
To find true freedom, it is not enough just to find our home in a role and work that we are doing in life. We can find the creativity that fulfills us and still become a prisoner of it if we get identified with the work or the role we are performing. There is another step to take and that is to separate our identity from anything we do and from any position, degree, or role that we play.

> *Not only have we been conditioned to play roles and fulfill expectations given to us by others but we are also taught to believe that the roles we play define whom we are. This becomes a perpetual prison.*

We adopt roles because we get something from them – approval, respect, recognition, love, appreciation, and perhaps also wealth but if we begin to become *identified* with our roles, it is as much a prison as being identified with our emotional child.

One of the most insidious roles we can abuse is that of "the guru", "the one who has the answers." A spiritual teacher I had years ago used to say that false gurus re-incarnate as cockroaches. He died a while ago. I hope he is not a cockroach running around somewhere. Often, Amana and I go on tour, lead five or six workshops in a row and then return to our home in Sedona. During that time, I receive heaps of positive (and sometimes negative) projections, praise, and even adulation. When I get home, it often feels as though someone turned off the ego-juice faucet. Until I became clear what was happening, I wasn't able to understand why I suddenly felt restless, moody, and lost. Fortunately, I am smart enough to know that getting that kind of ego-juice is not what life or at least what my life is about. I love it and I love the intensity of the role of being a workshop leader. But I am careful not to get hooked. And when I do, Amana reminds me.

Roles We Play in Relationship
We can also get trapped in roles when we are in a relationship. They give us security, identity, and predictability, but they kill love. Many of the couples we have known and worked with were destroying their relationship because one member of the couple was playing the role of the child, and the other, the parent. Or one is a student, the other is teacher, one is powerful and controlling, the other is weak and subservient.

CHAPTER 23: BREAKING OUT OF THE PRISON OF ROLES

Or one person is responsible and serious; the other is irresponsible, carefree, and childlike. This phenomenon is particularly prevalent between lovers but it is also occurs in most of our significant relationships - with parents, children, friends, colleagues at work, and authority figures.

There are other roles that we commonly play and become strongly identified with. A favorite is the role of the rescuer – the person who feels compelled to help, teach, heal, or advise others (often when it hasn't been asked for). There is nothing wrong with giving help but it does become a problem when we are attached to it. In our workshops, we often notice that participants compulsively go the aid of someone who is in pain. We have to remind them to allow the person to have his or her pain. One woman felt mortified when we suggested to her that actually it wasn't loving to take someone's pain away and perhaps she was doing it out of her own fear of feeling.

Another equally common role is that of the victim - often the angry victim. Our pain and suffering often causes us to become identified with feeling helpless and powerless. And, we may have learned to get attention through blaming, complaining or begging. Sometimes, we have become so accustomed to feeling and behaving as a victim that we can't imagine what life would be like without it. Sometimes, we ask people to notice how often they blame or complain and write down each time they catch themselves. It is amazing how much resistance that simple exercise provokes!

And then there is the role of the boss, the controller, or the tyrant. We can enjoy the power of that role and it also can have become so habitual that we no longer realize that it is a role. Many of those we work with have never been in a close relationship without being and feeling totally in control.

Behind the role of control and domination is tremendous fear of being vulnerable but it is not everyone who willingly and consciously wants to feel that vulnerability.

These roles compliment each other. A rescuer needs a victim and visa versa. A victim brings out the persecutor in most of us and a good tyrant so intimidates people around him or her that he invites the victim in them to come out. Parents are addicted to the role of a parent and abuse their children by not supporting them to grow up. Children are addicted to being children and resist growing up. A boss refuses to delegate responsibility because he or she believes that no one can do it better. But then he infantilizes those around him. And so on it goes.

Unconsciously, we stick to these complimentary roles because it maintains a certain status quo. It is safe and familiar. And it takes some courage to risk breaking out. In order to maintain a contract, we must compromise in some way but the fears of our emotional child can be so great that we accept the compromise willingly - at least for a while. The compromise involves agreeing overtly or covertly to not do anything that will rock the boat of the arrangement.

Breaking Out of The Role
The question is – how do we break out of our attachment to these roles? From my experience, there are three aspects to this journey.

First of all, we have to penetrate the lie of the ego.

> *We have to want something more in life that building up our ego - to see beyond the ego, to see that there is much more to life that living in an ego fulfilling state.*

This insight happened to me in two ways. First of all, it came as a result of meditation practice. Sitting in meditation, I could see so clearly that there was contentment far beyond what nourished the ego. I could also see that the ego fulfillment only nourishes a superficial part of my being. It didn't really go deep. But in meditation, I could sometimes touch a state that seemed to nourish me to my core and it had nothing to do with who I think I am.

Being in love and in a sustained and ever deepening relationship also gave me the insight that ego roles are not what life is really about. Living in my ego and being attached to my roles interfered with that love. It even blocked my ability to feel the preciousness of what we share and to go deeper in that space together. When I get attached to my role as a teacher and start to play that role unconsciously, our connection gets disturbed. It is as though I am moving from a delicate and refined state to a cruder and coarser state of being.

Sometimes, the hollowness of roles can come to us as a shock. One woman was sharing that when she divorced from her husband of thirty years, all of a sudden, she was no longer a wife, no longer an owner of a large house, and no longer a mother because her children were grown. It felt like the bottom had fallen out of her life. The so-called "midlife crisis" is little more than the realization that the roles we have been using to give us meaning in life are insubstantial and vacuous. It is existence (or God) saying "wake up, life is not about all of that!"

At that moment, we are given a choice. We can either collapse into depression or put our energy into seeking new and real meaning in life. We are part of a training in Sweden that is composed of ten weekly seminars each with different workshop leaders spread out over a year. It is a profound experience that radically changes peoples' life. Those who are motivated to make such a commitment are often people who have reached this kind of crisis in their lives and are seeking guidance for a new way. And they get it.

The second part of breaking out of our attachment to roles is being able to recognize and feel the roles when we are in it and getting lost in. One way to do that is to ask ourselves, "How much am I attached to this role?" "What do I get from being in this role?" "How would I feel if I am no longer in it?" "How would people see me if I am no longer this person?" Once we begin to ask ourselves these questions, we are already questioning them and more than halfway home.

In addition to becoming aware of the role and what the attachment is, we can also begin to *feel* the role. When I examine my roles closely, I start to feel the falseness of them. I can feel inside that there is something basically disconnected – both disconnected with myself and with others. The closer we are with someone, the stronger will be the feeling of disconnection when we are playing a role with that person.

And, each role has its own specific feel. Father or mother feels one way, child another, guru feels a certain way, disciple another and so on. Part of feeling the role is feeling how we relate to people and how they relate to us when we are in the role. Each role provokes a specific kind of behavior toward those who see us in the role and specific projections and behaviors in people who relate to us when we are in the role.

I can feel that strongly when I am in my "workshop leader" role. It is appropriate and an intrinsic part of my job in that role to understand what is expected of me and how people will treat me. To reject or complain about that would be childish and damaging to the people who come to us for that reason. But then it is a time to drop it when I am not in that position. A close friend of ours who is a world famous singer went to a party and felt strange because no one recognized her. She told us afterwards, with humor, "Don't they know who I *am*?!" Often when we are deeply attached to a role, we will play in even when we are with our intimate partner. We have another acquaintance that is a successful workshop leader and has never been able to drop this identity even with his girlfriends. Not surprisingly, they leave him after a while.

Which brings me to the third aspect of breaking our attachment to roles. *If we want to come out of this prison, we have to invite those closest to us to remind us when we forget and get lost.* Roles sabotage intimacy, but we can easily forget. Then we will need someone to remind us in a loving way, that we have gotten lost. Amana does that for me because I invite her to do so. I can't always tell when I get taken over and then her reminding me helps me to wake up. That wouldn't work if I wanted to stay attached. I don't and she knows it.

It isn't easy to drop our attachment to roles. But if we are sincere in our search for truth, we will see that roles are not who we are. There are times when it is totally appropriate and essential to play them and to play them impeccably. But once we have become attached, we can get lost into a world of ego-fulfillment and disconnection from people

Breaking Out of Roles
1. *Finding the courage to live what is true for us rather than what is expected.*
2. *Discovering that we are not the roles we play.*
3. *Recognizing how we are identified with a role.*

4. *Feeling how we feel inside when we are in a certain role.*
5. *Feeling how we relate with others and how they relate with us when we are a role.*
6. *Inviting someone close to us to remind us when we get lost in the role.*

> *You are not your name,*
> *You are not your body,*
> *You are not your mind,*
> *You are not your feelings,*
> *And you are not your heart.*
> *Anything that you have ever been identified with*
> *Has nothing to do with your reality.*
> *You are only a pure witness.*
> *I know this about you because I know this about me.*
> *Osho*

Exercises: Breaking Our Attachment to Roles
1. Make a list of three of the predominant roles you play in your life today- for instance - teacher, caretaker, healer, "spiritual person", boss, husband, wife, parent, child, disciple, guru, victim etc.
2. What feels good and what feels bad about each role? Does it fit for you to be in this role or it is something you are doing to please others?
3. What kind of ego gratification do you get from each role?
4. What would it feel like if you lost this role?

5. How would it change what other people think of you if you lost the role?
6. What would be the benefits of not having the role?

Chapter 24:

RELATING AND THE EMOTIONAL CHILD

Luigi was motivated to do our training in Italy because he had decided that women are all castrating bitches and he wanted to find a way to deal with this situation. It is not at all surprising that an Italian man should come to this conclusion but Luigi had had enough. He wanted to learn how to deal with women, only he had great difficulty seeing that the women were not the problem. He was.

To the emotional child looking at the other person, every woman can be castrating or controlling and every man can be a dominating male chauvinist pig. In fact, there are basically few problems with the other person or even with the relationship; the problem is that we need to be clear who is looking.

When we are unconsciously looking out through the eyes of our emotional child, problems are inevitable. We explain to people that when they enter into a relationship without much understanding, it is often shame or abandonment "going shopping". The shame wants approval and validation; the abandonment wants reassurance of eternal presence and devotion, the mistrust wants the other person never to betray our trust.

Who Is Relating?
For a long time, I was attracted to relating techniques to help myself or people I worked with connect more intimately. They can be very helpful and we actually use some in our work. But

basically, there is a deeper understanding needed before any of these techniques do any good.

The key question is - who is relating.

Are we coming from our emotional child or from a place inside which has enough inner space to be with the disappointments and miscommunications that come up without getting lost in blame, endless processing, or conflict? Are we coming from a space of panic and lost in the narrow focus of our own needs and wants or are we able to take in the relationship with a wide-angle lens with feelings and caring for the other person?

> *Fundamentally, it is not techniques, agreements, and commitments, or trying to be different that make our relationships work. What makes them work is bringing awareness to our emotional child.*

When we are unconsciously in our emotional child state of mind, no techniques or agreements or improvements will ever make any difference. Behind the fancy words or spiritual concepts will be lurking all our expectations, reactiveness, hopes, fantasies, and frustration.

With a deeper understanding for the behaviors and feelings of the emotional child, we can know what space we are coming from. Often, I can see myself moving automatically into an emotional child frame and I know that if I act it out from that space, there will be conflict. Feeling when the emotional child takes over allows me now often to make the choice not to act it out. Or having started down the road of acting out, I catch it very quickly.

Sometimes, I get moody and irritable and nothing seems to go right. I feel like a horrible failure with nothing valuable to give and life seems meaningless. Everything and everyone around bugs me. It is a mood and I know, even in the thick of it, that it will pass. At those moments, it is easy to react on other people with demands, expectations, or frustrations and to feel disappointed and unloved if they are not there for me.

Expecting others to be there for us is not realistic. It is better to be with ourselves and just watch. In fact, the idea of someone being there for us is magical thinking. It is a miracle when people are there for themselves. Nevertheless, it is not comfortable when we don't get what we want and of course our emotional child wants someone to take the anxiety away. But they can't.

It is not the Commitment but who is making the Commitment
People may attempt to bring consciousness into their relating by making agreements. Again, we have to ask, who is making the agreement? If it is the emotional child, the agreements won't hold. For instance, one of the most common agreements we encounter is for two people in a relationship who agree not to have other lovers. If this comes from an understanding that both persons have reached as a result of their own individual inner search, then there is no need to make an agreement; it is simply an understanding that they share.

But if this comes, as it often seems to, from one or both wanting to please or placate the other or to repress something, then it only lasts for a while. What can happen instead is that we make such an agreement but it is later broken with secrecy and guilt. We have seen this countless times in our work and I was there once myself. Wanting or pretending to be somewhere that is not true for us never works.

Furthermore, we don't change because of agreements. We change as a result of awareness. We can't make the other person or ourselves more open and willing to share, more accountable, and responsible or more honest simply because we want or agree to be that way. People often make a contract about spending time together and it can be motivated by fear and guilt. This usually comes from a situation where one person is getting frustrated because he or she does not get enough time with the other. I was frequently in this situation in the past as the one who was too occupied doing other things. And often I agreed to spend more time with my lover but it was coming out of fear. At that time, I simply liked to do the things I was doing alone better than relating. I didn't know enough about intimacy to enjoy sharing non-structured time and anyway, I am a doer. Now, it has changed partly because my relationship with Amana is so free of demands and expectations, partly because I have slowly (very slowly) learned to relax more and mostly because I enjoy spending time with Amana.

The more sensitive we become to our wounds, the more sensitive we become with those of the other person as well. Becoming sensitive to shock, shame, and the fears of abandonment soften us. It's hard to shame someone when you know what if feels like. Once we know about shock, we can recognize it in the eyes, facial expressions, and body posture of the other person also. It's harder to leave someone abruptly when we know our own fears of separating or being abandoned.

And this sensitivity also applies to the smaller things. It's hard to be unaccountable when we know how it feels when someone is not accountable with us. We know what it feels like when someone tells us he or she is going to do something and then doesn't. We know what it feels like to be lied to. A close friend of mine recently shared with me that he discovered that his lover of seven years was having a secret affair with someone for over a year without his knowing about it. This kind of dishonesty is not only very painful but it can only happen when two people are not being present with each other. When there is presence, each one feels the slightest disturbance or lack of truthfulness between them. The deeper we enter into intimacy, the greater our fears are. We cannot protect another from his or her fears, but it isn't loving to provoke them either.

The same is true for respecting each other's boundaries. It becomes a shared understanding that love and trust deepens when we let the other person be. One of the strongest lessons that I have had to learn is that my beloved's emotional and spiritual growth is none of my business. That part inside of me who wants to fix, improve, and direct people does not do great things for improving intimacy. In fact, we need to get some perspective from our "controller" if we wish to deepen love and trust.

For example, Peter has been doing our work for several years. He shared at the last workshop that he did with us that he was upset that he still did not have a love affair that worked. But he does not see that he reacts impulsively and sometimes violently when he doesn't feel seen by another person. He is demanding and entitled and still feels that women want to possess him. In our groups, I sometimes use an expression from Tennessee Williams's play, *"Cat on a Hot Tin Roof."* The main character, played by Paul Newman, who is an alcoholic, would say that he could only stop drinking when "he heard the click". Peter will not be able to have a harmonious relationship until he "has heard the click" - when he is able to have some space from his demanding emotional child and recognize what he is doing that is driving women away from him.

Our emotional child would like the other person to share our point of view - on everything. Not just with our lover but with everyone. The emotional child in us wants homogeneity in order to feel comfortable. It is shocking to our emotional child when we discover that someone just doesn't think or behave as we do or as we think he or she should. We gather around us people who share our point of view in all kinds of ways - politically and socially and we judge those who don't.

That may work in the Rotary Club but it doesn't work very well with intimacy. And, actually we often attract people who are different from us so that we can move out of familiarity and challenge our fears. The closer we come to someone, the sooner our emotional child will have to face disappointment when he or she discovers that the other is different and often in very fundamental ways. To our child, that may bring up anxiety, anger, and even despair.

The Emotional Child Does Not Relate Consciously
To relate consciously, we have to put the emotional child to the side and look clearly at what understandings and points of view we share and which we don't. What do we have in common and what don't we have in common, noticing what goals, desires, values, and lifestyle we share. We have to do this with everyone of our relationships and in all areas of life - looking at how our concepts of intimacy are similar and differ, what we share or not share in how we enjoy to entertain ourselves, how we like to spend our time, how

we like to make love, how we like to eat, at our standards of cleanliness, at our spirituality and so on. The closer we come, the more important become even the smallest aspects of sharing life together. Basically, we have to begin to see the other person for who he or she is and prepare ourselves for being disappointed each time our emotional child feels that there is no homogeneity.

When we take away the veil of the emotional child, many things become clear. One is that even though we are wounded, frightened and insecure, no one can meet the irrational needs of our emotional child. When these needs are not met, it may provoke a disturbance inside. To have intimacy, we simply have to let go of our magical thinking and face the fears that arise. Our friendships and love affairs can be a wonderful arena to learn this art. We can embrace one another recognizing that we can be sensitive to the other person's fears and pain without rescuing the other person from these feelings.

Also, our relationships are an excellent arena for teaching us to set limits. When we have learned to respect ourselves, we rarely get invaded. Finally, we can learn that we don't need permission to take the space we need; we only have to willing to face our fears of rejection and disapproval. Love and trust flowers when we recognize that we are basically and fundamentally alone. In that atmosphere, everything is possible. Love brings deep sensitivity to each other. In spite of our fears and past hurts related to sex, when another person loves us, he or she will understand and respect our fears in this area. Love grows naturally with awareness; we don't have to learn rules and techniques. We only have to make an effort to know who is in charge at any given moment - is it our emotional child or is it our centered stated of consciousness?

Recognizing Our State of Consciousness

The Child State	*The Mature Adult State*
Projection	*Seeing the Other Clearly*
Blame Other for Moods	*Take Responsibility for Moods*
Insensitive to Other	*Respect for Other*
Ask Permission for Space	*Take the Space We Need*
No Limits or Excessive Limits	*Set Limits With Clarity*
Unclear Commitments	*Commitment Based on Wisdom*
Other is the Savior	*Take Responsibility for Fear & Pain*
Expect Homogeneity	*Expect and Enjoy Differences*
Rules and Commitments	*Shared Understandings*

Moving From The Child to The Mature Adult State

We find that there are eight qualities that help us move from the emotional child way to relating to the mature adult way of relating. They are eight basic points that serve as a kind of blueprint for conscious relating.

1. Willing to Be Honesty
Once we become more aware of our incredible sensitivity and vulnerability, it is easier to understand that to open we need

honesty. When we are holding something back from the person we are intimate with, whether it is a lover or a friend, that person will feel it. Even if we are not aware that there is something we are being dishonest about, at a deeper place, the other person will feel it and pull away often without even knowing why. One startling example comes to my mind from a recent workshop.

A man was participating in a workshop and came to me for an individual session. He shared with me that he was having an affair but had not told his wife. He was convinced that she didn't have any idea that it was happening and that it did not affect their relating. Yet he somehow felt that they could not really come close. I told him that until he was honest, their relationship would never go deeper. After the session, Amana and I happened to meet his wife whom we had known from an earlier group. She thanked us and told us that after the group, something had totally changed in their relating. In a sense, one thing we really owe each other is our honesty. This is something that we have some control over. We can decide to be honest!

2. Willing to Drop Power Games

Our strategies of control, manipulation, or revenge are well-developed devices to get the other person to do what we want or to make them suffer for a hurt we feel. We have been using these methods since childhood and each of us has his or her favorites. These games are habitual and automatic but they sabotage intimacy. We also wait for the other to drop his or her power games first and only then do we feel safe to drop ours. That is just another power game. If we take full responsibility to become aware of our games, we can choose to drop them. It is our job to identify and feel the games that we play and to observe how they destroy the love that we want. It is our job to take the risk to drop them.

3. Willing to Exposing Our Fears and Insecurities.

It takes a risk to share something that can give the other person the ability to hurt us. But what are we protecting, after all? The other person already knows what we are afraid of or insecure about, if not consciously then intuitively. When we are hiding a fear, the other person may not know the specific event or events, which may have caused this fear, but he or she almost certainly can sense the fear. Whenever we ask people to expose some fears or insecurities in a group, they are usually amazed that the other people already know about them. Also, when we share something that we have hidden, it loses its charge and allows us to come closer.

4. Willing to Stop Trying to Change the Other Person

When we let go of trying to change the other person, we are forced to feel our pain of abandonment when the other is not how we want or expect him or her to be. Another aspect of this is that once we let go of the need to change the other, we begin to love and accept them for all of their imperfections. It might be accurate to say that we actually love the other person's imperfections. In a recent group in Italy, after we mentioned this point, one person commented: "Oh, so that means that I simply say to my wife, I love you because you are ugly, stupid, lazy, old, and boring." We suggested that he had not exactly understood the point.

5. Being Willing to Stand Up For Ourselves

There will be times when we have to assert ourselves when we feel that we have been treated in a disrespectful way. This is an important lesson, a way of retrieving a lost part of us. Intimate relating forces us to take this risk otherwise we will collapse into depression, hopelessness, and resentment.

6. Willing to Receive Feedback
As we come closer to another person, if we are not able to take feedback, we shut down one of the most important ways to learn from intimacy. Relationship is a mirror and the deeper the love, the stronger the mirror. Our words and behavior impact those close to us and if we can remain continually open to how they feel with us, we begin to understand ourselves much more deeply.

7. Willing to Commit In Spite of Frustration
Intimacy is risky. We never know what will happen if we open and allow ourselves to feel again. It is a choice because when frustrations and disappointments arise, as they always will, we have to resist the impulse to run away. The ability to hang in there is a choice we have made inside when we realize that love takes work, commitment, and perseverance. Not all relationships are meant to last and sometimes it is totally right to end one. But there is no relationship, which will always be smooth sailing.

8. Cultivating Inner Space
Whenever someone would ask our spiritual Master a question about relationships, his answer invariably came back to this same point. Love is based on meditation, inner space. The only problem with our love stories is that we simply do not have enough meditation. He would explain that he has been saying this to us for twenty years but we never listen. Meditation is

at the end of our shopping list. And by meditation, he meant inner space, the ability to contain discomfort and to be present to the moment. It is important to put it at the top of our shopping list.

> *"The capacity to be alone is the capacity of love.*
> *It may sound paradoxical to you but it is not.*
> *It is an existential truth; only.*
> *Those who are capable of being alone*
> *Are capable of love, of sharing,*
> *Of going to the deepest core of the other person –*
> *Without possessing, without becoming dependent on the other,*
> *Because they are not addicted to the other."*
> *Osho*

Exercises:
1. Recognizing Your State of Consciousness in Relating

When you enter or are in a relationship, ask yourself, "Am I relating right now from the space of a child or a mature adult?"

    a. ***The child space*** is characterized by demands, drama, power games, dishonesty, expectations, continual disappointments, strategies of control, and manipulation, insensitivity, and disrespect for the other person, and wanting to change the other person.

b. ***The mature adult space*** sees the other person as he or she is, is respectful both for one's own needs and those of the other, recognizes that the other person is not there to rescue you, communicates clearly and honestly and is not trying to change the other person.

2. Practicing Becoming More Honest

Take a look at your most intimate relationships in your life today.

    a. In what way are you not honest with that person – what secrets are you withholding?
    b. How does it feel inside when you are being dishonest?
    c. How does it affect your relating?
    d. What would be your fear if you were honest?
    e. What would you need to say to feel more honest?

3. Dropping Power Games

Examine in what ways you are defending yourself and creating distance in your most intimate relationships.

    a. What specific behaviors are you doing? Blaming, attacking, isolating, needing to be right, talking behind someone's back, taking revenge, playing the victim or the rescuer.
    b. What is the fear behind these behaviors?
    c. How could you drop these behaviors?

4. Exposing Fears and Insecurities

Picking the most significant persons in your life, ask yourself:

a. How is it for you to expose your fears and insecurities to this person?
b. What are your judgments about doing so with this person?
c. What are your fears?

5. Wanting to Change the Other Person
a. Picking the most significant persons in your life,
b. In what ways would you like this person to change?
c. What happens in the relating when this person hears or feels that you would like him or her to change?
d. How does it feel if he or she were never to change?
e. If the person never changes, would you still want to be with this person?

6. Opening to Feedback
Picking the most important person in your life, ask them,
a. "What would help you to feel closer and safer with me?"
b. "What do I do or say that makes you pull away from me?"

7. Cultivating Inner Space
What could you do in your life to help you bring more inner sense of calm and peace? Walking in nature, dancing, meditating, doing yoga, etc. Pick one of these resources and make a commitment to do it for at least twenty minutes a day for 21 days.

Chapter 25:

LIVING IN BALANCE

In our emotional child state of mind, we seldom appreciate our beauty and our natural qualities. It is blocked by shame. For example, Diana, a participant from one of our trainings, is a warm, loving, and playful person with a unique brightness and intelligence. She endears people to her immediately. But Diana does not think she has any special qualities. She thinks she is just a fat, boring, sad person. She is so identified with her shamed self-image that she has trouble seeing that there is anything else. In some way, most of us have some of Diana's problem. We can easily become identified with our shame and forget what is valuable, beautiful, and special about us.

Yet when we begin to become aware that we are unique and special, we also begin to break the identification with our shame. As Diana progressed through the training, she became aware that there is more to her than what her emotional child thinks. She began to appreciate her own gifts and qualities and the unique way that these flow out of her. Until we are becoming aware of these unique qualities, we wonder how we can contribute to life - what is it that gives us a sense of belonging and value?

Our Worth is not based on What We Do
Like a seed planted in soil, if the seed is watered, fertilized and cared for, it flowers. If it isn't, it just lies dormant waiting to

flower or can even die. We may have received the message that our value as a person depended on what we do and we learned to measure our self-worth on how well and how successfully we express our gifts. Often we are given a confusing mixed message. We are told that we are loved no matter what we do but underneath, we know that all that is really valued is success and achievement. That was clearly the message that I got. As a result of this message, we grow with the belief that it is what we do, not who we are that matters. There is no space and no value attached to being - only to doing.

I have always thought that parents face an extremely difficult job when it comes to supporting their children's gifts. How to give a child the strength and confidence to persevere and to overcome obstacles and disappointments in the pursuit of his or her creativity and yet at the same time show him or her that by relaxing and appreciating ourselves, our flowering will happen? My father had to overcome the handicap of being Jewish in a world that, at the time he was growing up, was strongly anti-Semitic and also a handicap of being extremely near-sighted. Both gave him a powerful sense of drive but he became convinced that the only way to succeed was to compare and compete.

He buried his sensitivity under the intense burden of proving his worth. It often seems that we have no choice but to push, control, and compare and struggle to make it. But our self-expression then becomes an agonizing and tense struggle between striving and collapsing. This dilemma creates a deep disturbance and pain inside. We have no idea that our flowering could just be a natural and spontaneous outpouring of our gifts and qualities. If we do succeed, we give the credit to our jungle skills rather than to grace. It is hard for us to imagine what it would be like if the development and expression of our qualities did happen in an atmosphere of grace.

The Negative Conditioning of our Qualities
1. *You are no good or not good enough.*
2. *There is no one there to guide you to find out who you are.*
3. *Your value depends on what you do.*
4. *Life is a jungle where you have to compete and struggle to shine*

The conditioning which most of us receive in relation to our qualities is in strong contrast to the stories of spiritual masters guiding their disciples in the development of their gifts. When I first went to India to be with my Master twenty years ago, I had my mind set on being a therapist in his community. I loved the idea of combining therapy with meditation and thought that nothing could be more wonderful than dong what I loved to do in this inspiring setting. People were coming from all over the world by the hundreds to grow and learn. Plus, those who were working with people in this place were doing a new and original kind of work combining all the latest transpersonal methods with meditation under personal guidance from an enlightened Master. I had left a budding therapy practice in California to fulfill this dream.

When I started to work in the commune, I had every expectation of rapidly becoming one of this elite group. Instead, I spent five years doing nearly everything else – washing dishes, cleaning resident's rooms, doing carpentry and construction, driving buses, practicing medicine

- everything but what I wanted to do. I went through agony. I did not want to leave the community because it was the only place I wanted to be. Yet I had to watch my closest friends doing precisely what I wanted to do and 1 was afraid that I would never fulfill my "creative destiny". Every year, I would write a letter to my Master asking him if he thought I was ready. Each time, he replied that I was fine where I was.

Finally, after I had given up all hope of my dream becoming fulfilled, I got a message to start working as a therapist. Strangely enough, I had finally become content in what I was doing. Now, I am indescribably grateful for that painful time. I can see that it was a kind of training period that taught me how to be more human. I recognize that the success of my work is more a result of those five years of waiting than of all the years that I spent in training.

Also, it built a determination in me. Recently a friend asked me what happened to my passion to be a therapist during all the years that I waited. I thought about it for a moment and then answered that it made me realize that nothing was going to stop me from fulfilling my dream. It kindled a fire inside that took me through all the disappointments, failures, rejections, and discouragements I have encountered along the way

Tuning The Inner and Outer Visions
The Master recognizes the disciple's gifts but he gives him trials that build his meditation, his strength of character, his ability to persevere, his trust, his compassion, and his patience. My Master has always made it clear that our skill is not who we are and our worth as a person has nothing to do with what we excel in. Our gift is the natural unfolding

of our attunement to life and the development of our own inner sense of excellence. Success or failure is irrelevant, what matters is only tuning the expression of our gifts into the harmony and flow of existence.

What matters is only the deepening of our meditation - our awareness, our ability to be in the moment, and to trust in with our gifts. In fact, our skill is just a laboratory for our meditation, nothing more. All skills are equal. What differs is only the degree of commitment, tuning, and presence. Whatever we enjoy to do and have natural talent at doing is the same whether it is gardening, martial arts, flute playing, food preparation, healing, or preparing tea.

When we lack this tuning with our own qualities, we may find ourselves in a struggle to achieve for others and to weigh our achievement according to how we compare to others. This is a painful and never-ending endeavor, which obviously takes us away from our center. Once we start to recognize the qualities and gifts that have always been there, we also begin to see that their value does not depend on comparison or even appreciation. It is just who we are.

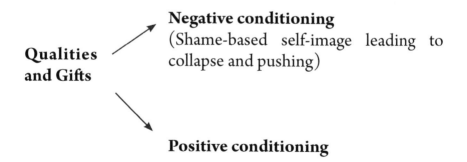

(Healthy self-image based on attunement, meditation, and appreciating our uniqueness)

*"It is simply a fact that everybody is unique
And everybody has a certain individuality.
We just have to drop ideas of how people should be,
And we have to replace it with a philosophy that
However people are, they are beautiful.
The whole humanity can be such a loving
And rejoicing place
If we can accept people as they are."*
Osho

Exercises: The Flowering of Your Gifts

1. Sit down and close your eyes. Take a few moments to tune inside. Imagine that you are sitting opposite someone who deeply loves you and sees your gifts and uniqueness even better than you do. What would this person say about you? You may want to write this down.
2. In the flowering of your qualities, how have you been affected by competition and comparison? How have you dealt with them? What specific steps have you taken to flower in your creativity? How do these steps reflect your beliefs about competition and comparison?

3. Now imagine a world without competition and comparison. How would your qualities flower in this world?

Conclusion

There is a story of a student who went to the Zen master, Bankei with a question.

"Master," he said, "I have an uncontrollable anger. How do I learn to manage it?"

"Show me this anger," the master replied, "It sounds fascinating."

"I cannot show it to you because it is not here right now."

"Well then, bring it to me when you have it."

"But I cannot bring it to you just when I happen to have it," protested the student, "It arises unexpectedly, and I would surely lose it before I brought it to you."

"In that case," said Bankei, "it cannot be a part of your true nature. If it were, you could show it to me at any time. When you were born, you did not have it so it must come to you from the outside."

We might say the same about not just anger but all other aspects of the emotional child as well. They are not part of our true nature. Yet we live as though they were. What would it be like if we begin to realize that this is only something which we received from the outside? It is not who we are and we do not have to live our life as if it were. We might wonder what life is like and what would it be to love if our emotional child did not run us? What happens when we have some distance from our expectations, blame, reactions, and all of our strategies to manipulate and control others? What is love like without the drama that all of this provokes? What happens to our life when we have some space from our push to achieve or from our incessant self-judgment? Does love become boring and empty? Without push to motivate ourselves does our creativity never develop? Without the watchful eye of our inner judge, do we end up as degenerate psychopaths?

These certainly were questions that I have had. But I can recognize that the feeling that I had to push and struggle came from my mind, from the fears and mistrust of my conditioning. I recognize that the past clings to me in the form of all of the behaviors and feelings that live inside my emotional child. They are familiar and secure. They have given me identity. Without them, I easily felt lost. But with them, my life becomes a disaster.

Disidentifying from the emotional child is a process that takes patience and perseverance. It is a process that takes remembering – remembering that the feelings, thoughts, and behavior we have described, come from the emotional child. In consciousness, I can separate from the child inside and see that it is only a part of the mind created by negative conditioning. That does not mean that I must deny that this part is inside of me but I can appreciate that it is based on the past. We are, as Buddha said, sufficient unto ourselves.

The love I share with Amana is not based on our needing each other. It is based on sharing our consciousness and on our respect for each other as two separate beings. We can acknowledge that each of us has an emotional child inside with mistrust, shame, fear, anger, and grief that sometimes behaves unconsciously with reactions, expectations, or insensitivity. But the emotional child does not create the love. On the contrary, it sabotages it when I am not conscious of it.

When the emotional child does not run our life, our life develops a different quality. It becomes much more cool. Mostly, the heat and drama we create in our life come from the fears, shame, and abandonment fears of the emotional child. As we become more centered inside and more comfortable with our own aloneness, drama loses its grip. But rather than lessen the love we can share and the life we can live, it deepens it.

I could not have imagined years ago that my creativity and my ability to "make it" could happen without my pusher. I feared that I would simply surrender to my insecurities. A teacher that supported and guided me in my creative development would often say to me, "Krish, how can you possibly give existence a chance to prove to you that everything happens at the right time and in the right way, when you are always pushing and doing." It has been one my greatest challenges not to allow my ambition and my fears run me in this area. Yet I can see clearly from past experience that things turn out well even without my constant interference. Removing the compulsive emotional child from my creative expression is a huge relief. The gifts are there and will come out in a beautiful flowing way even when I don't "make" things happen. Slowly I see that my pusher does not deserve the credit.

Without the judge scrutinizing my every move, I am free to relax into living my life naturally, learning to trust my intelligence, my sensitivity and my interior motivation to grow and find myself.

All of these characters - the pusher, the judge, the needy child arise in the mind in response to fear. At one time, we believed that they are needed. But they have outgrown their usefulness and linger as automatic, unconscious remnants of an earlier time. With awareness and compassion, we can gently set them aside and return to our true nature – trusting that we have all that we need to live in a much more natural and spontaneous fashion.

As I gain more and more distance from the thoughts, behaviors, and feelings of my emotional child, I am able to connect more strongly with my centeredness, my natural gifts, my compassion, and my heartfulness and inner silence. These aspects of my being have not always been given the credit they deserve. But the more I recognize them, the deeper I relax. I accept that it is a journey that in some ways, I have only begun. But the journey has become joyful. I react less often and when I do, it can forgive myself. Fear, disturbance, anger, shame still arise, but I can watch them and they pass. I am with the person I love more than anything in the world and I am deeply passionate about the work we do together. I wish the same for everyone who reads this book.

Much love, Krishnananda (and Amana)

*"I don't say anything to you about heaven or hell,
Punishment or reward. I simply say to you:
Go on dying to the past
So it is not a burden on your head.
And do not live in the future
Which is not yet.
Concentrate your whole energy here and now.
Pour it in this moment,
With totality, with as much intensity as
you can manage…*

There is nothing to be feared.
Existence is your mother.
You are part of it.
It cannot drown you, it cannot destroy you.
The more you know it, the more you will feel nourished;
The more you know it, the more you will feel blessed;
The more you will be."
Osho

Selected References

A.H. Almaas, **_Diamond Heart Book 1 Elements of Real in Man_**, Diamond Books, Berkeley, California 1987

A. H. Almaas, **_The Point of Existence - Transformations of Narcissism in Self Realization_**, Diamond Books, Berkeley, California 1996

Bader and Pearson, **_The Quest of the Mythical Mate – A Developmental Approach to Diagnosis and Treatment in Couples Therapy_**, Brunner Mazel, New York 1988

John Bradshaw, **_Homecoming - Reclaiming and Championing Your Inner Child_** Bantam Books, New York 1990

Forrest Carter, **_The Education of Little Tree_**, University of New Mexico Press Albuquerque, New Mexico 1976

Erik Erikson, **_Childhood and Society_**, Norton, New York 1993

Selma H. Frieberg, **_The Magic Years - Understanding and Handling The Problems of Early Childhood_**, Charles Scribner's Sons, New York 1959

Greenberg and Mitchell, **_Object Relations in Psychoanalytic Theory_**, Harvard University Press Cambridge, Massachusetts 1983

George Gurdjieff, **_Meetings With Remarkable Men_**, Dutton New York, 1969

Judith Lewis Herman, M.D. *__Trauma and Recovery The Aftermath of Violence – from Domestic Abuse and Political Terror__*, Basic Books 1992

Harville Hendricks, *__Conscious Loving - The Journey of Co-Commitment__*, Bantam Books 1990

Bert Hellinger, *__Love's Hidden Symmetry - What Makes Love Work in Relationship__*, Zeig, Tucker and Co., Phoenix, Arizona 1998

Karen Homey, *__Neurosis and Human Growth - The Struggle Toward Self-Realization__*, Norton, New York 1991

Margaret Mahler, *__The Psychological Birth of the Human Infant__*, Basic Books, New York 1975

Osho, *__Glimpses of A Golden Childhood__*, Rebel Publishing House, Cologne, Germany 1990

Osho, *__The Path of the Mystic__*, Rebel Publishing House Cologne, Germany 1987

Osho, *__The New Dawn__*, Rebel Publishing House Cologne, Germany 1988

Osho, *__The Razor's Edge__*, Rebel Publishing House, Cologne, Germany 1990

Osho, *__Seeds of Wisdom__*, Rebel Publishing House, Cologne, Germany 1991

Stone and Winkelman, *__Embracing Each Other – Relationship as Teacher, Healer and Guide__*, Nataraj Publications, Los Angeles 1993

Judith Viorst, *__Necessary Losses - The Loves, Illusions, Dependencies and Impossible Expectations That All of Us__*

Have to Give up in Order to Grow, Ballantine Books, New York 1987

Barry and Janae Weinhold, Ph.D., ***Breaking Free of the Co-Dependency Trap***, Stillpoint Publishing, Walpole, NH, 1989

Barry and Janae Weinhold, Ph.D., ***The Flight From Intimacy – Healing Your Relationships of Counter-dependency – the Other Side of Co-Dependency***, New World Library, Novato, California, 2008

Steven Wolinsky, ***Trances People Live – Healing Approaches in Quantum Psychology***, Bramble Books, New York 1991

Eiji Yoshikawa, ***Musashi - An Epic Novel of the Samurai***, Era Kodansha International, Tokyo 1980

Biography:

Krishnanda and Amana Trobe have been leading seminars together since 1995. Their work has developed out of their experience being in a love relationship for many years and inspired by the teachings of a spiritual master.

Krishnanda is a psychiatrist educated and trained at Harvard and the University of California.

Amana is a therapist, certified in Cranio-Sacral Balancing and also trained in Counseling, Light Puncture and Inner Child Work.

Other books that Krishnananda and Amana have written describing their work and experiences include, *"Face to Face with Fear- Transcending Fear into Love"*, *"When Trust Fails and How We Recover It – Learning to Trust Yourself and Others"* and *"When Sex Becomes Intimate – How Sexuality Changes As Your Relationship Deepens."* The books have been translated into Spanish, German, Turkish, Italian, Russian, French and Swedish.

When not leading workshops around the world, they are at home in Sedona, Arizona.

Made in United States
Orlando, FL
26 May 2024

47217444R00178